EDITOR
Nik Samson
editor@100-biker.co.uk

ART EDITOR
Gareth Evans
gareth@jazzpublishing.co.uk
Telephone: 01244 663400 ext. 204

GRAPHIC DESIGNER
Lindsay Burdekin
lindsay.burdekin@jazzpublishing.co.uk
Telephone: 01244 663400 ext. 226

PRODUCTION MANAGER
Justine Hart
justine@jazzpublishing.co.uk
Telephone: 01244 663400 ext. 235

ACCOUNTS & ADMIN MANAGER
Emma McCrindle
accounts@jazzpublishing.co.uk
Telephone: 01244 663400 ext. 207

ADMINISTRATION
Jan Schofield
jan@jazzpublishing.co.uk
Telephone: 01244 663400 ext. 219
Katie-Marie Challinor
katie@jazzpublishing.co.uk
Telephone: 01244 663400 Ext. 220

CREDIT CONTROL
Pam Coleman
pam@jazzpublishing.co.uk
Telephone: 01244 663400 ext. 215

ADVERTISING ENQUIRIES
Louise Chamberlain-Jones
advertising@100-biker.co.uk
Telephone: 01244 663400 ext. 317

CIRCULATION & PROMOTIONS
Katy Cuffin
katy@jazzpublishing.co.uk
Telephone: 01244 663400 Ext. 237

PUBLISHER
David Gamble
david@jazzpublishing.co.uk
Telephone: 01244 663400

MANAGING DIRECTOR
Stuart Mears
stuart@jazzpublishing.co.uk
Telephone: 01244 663400

PRINTED BY
Warners Midlands plc

CONTRIBUTORS
John Brandwood, Asa Infinity Studios, Clinton Smith Rip, Nik Samson, Larry Harris, Steve Beachill, Bazza, Irish Paul,
Garry Laurence, Spindle, Pc, Derek De Reuck, Guy 'Elvis' Simons, Tony 'Buck' Buckingham, Mr Pk, Phil Piper

CONTENTS

074 The Confederate

080 Perfectly Created

084 White Magic

090 Old English Custom

096 Fat Attack

100 For Yoffi

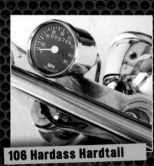
106 Hardass Hardtail

110 The Shadow

114 Last Minute Wonder

120 Strike True II

126 The Mantis

134 The Genuine Article

138 Hot Rod

142 The Best HD in the UK

148 Attitude

152 Fat Custom

INTRODUCTION

WORDS: NIK SAMSON

Thanks to television programmes such as Discovery Channel's 'American Chopper' and the like, today just about everyone and their dog knows what a custom motorcycle is.

What they may not know, though, is the words 'custom motorcycle' don't necessarily mean 'chopper' – a custom bike doesn't have to be a chopper. In fact, looking back through custom biking history what the guys who started the scene called a 'chopper' isn't quite the same thing as what we associate the word with today.

You see, when the breed was first envisaged back in the late '40s, 'choppers' were bikes, usually Harley-Davidsons or Indians, that their owners 'chopped' in order to make them

lighter and, therefore, faster and more able to hold their own against the smaller-engined, but more quicker and better handling imported British bikes that were starting to come into the US of A. They took off as many of the big bulky components forever associated with traditional American motorcycles – heavy front mudguards, bulbous headlights and tinware, twin fuel and oil tanks, massive dual seats and all-enclosing rear mudguards – forever changing the look of them and creating the first real custom bikes as we know them.

Then, by the time the Sixties and the 'Flower Power' with its drugs and free love culture came around, custom bikes began to change from out and out speedsters into an expression of their riders' personal freedoms and beliefs and, when the ◐

We here at 100% Biker, though, are aware that a custom bike doesn't have to be a chopper and so we've put together this book, 'Legends', to show you some the best UK custom bikes from our long history.

554
UXE

From seminal matt blackers that have gone on to influence a whole generation of post apocalyptic road warriors' machines to the some of the most technically innovative techno-choppers every built.

film 'Easy Rider' came out in 1969, the 'chopper' as it was now known was cemented in people's minds as a weird-looking motorcycle with long forks, high handlebars, intricate paint schemes and more bling than

in the most expensive jewellers' window.

We here at *100% Biker*, though, are aware that a custom bike doesn't have to be a chopper and so we've put together this book, 'Legends', to show you some of the best UK custom bikes from our long history. The bikes in here aren't all choppers in the strictest sense, although the general public might lump them all together under that name, but they are a celebration of the skill and diversity of the British custom bike builder. We firmly believe, you see, that British folk build the best custom bikes in the world – maybe not the blingiest, maybe not the most expensive, we leave that to people in other countries,

but definitely the most imaginative, the most ground-breaking, the most thought-provoking and the most copied. Remember, imitation is the sincerest form of flattery, isn't it?

In 'Legends' we bring you bikes from both ends of the custom spectrum – from seminal matt blackers that have gone on to influence a whole generation of post apocalyptic road warriors' machines to some of the most technically innovative techno-choppers ever built. Add to them traditional choppers, bikes built on a budget so low that our American cousins couldn't buy a mudguard with and, of course, archetypal British café racers and you'll see exactly why we reckon that us Brits do it best. And long may we continue to do so! ⊗

T-BOB DUCATI

WE'RE ALL AWARE THESE DAYS OF THE GIANTS OF THE UK CUSTOM BIKE BUILDING SCENE – THE GUYS/COMPANIES WHOSE NAMES ARE ALMOST NEVER OUT OF THE MAGAZINES.

Laydeez n' gennulmen, let me introduce you to a builder who is a regular in the British bike media – this is Mr Roger Allmond of Allmond Cycle Design and the ab-so-lute-ly drop dead gorgeous motorcycle here in front of you is his latest and greatest creation - T-Bob.

T-Bob came about as a result of his deciding to stop playing at bike building and get into it seriously. Three years ago, he sold his engineering business and went back to university to study design (where, he says, he met some unbelievably insular and pretentious w*nkers) and, having gained the relevant qualifications, set about designing and building the bike before you with a vengeance. He sold a big old house that he'd renovated and bought a smaller one with a workshop so that he could work from home. With his new base of operations set up, he was casting about for ideas when his eye lit upon an old 916 Ducati motor that he had sat under a bench. That was it! His inspiration was staring him straight in the face. Everyone builds radical bikes around vee-twin engines these days, but they all, almost to a man, use Harley-Davidson engines or derivatives thereof. Roger decided that he would build one around one of the other famous vee-twin brand's motors, but not just around an ageing sportsbike motor. No, he had far loftier aspirations than that ... He approached Ducati UK and spoke to their PR guy, Luke Plummer, and arranged a meeting. He went down there with a sheaf of drawings and, once Luke and Ducati had

seen with their own eyes that he wasn't some small-timer with his head in the clouds, they agreed to provide him with a bike to use as a base for his creation. They gave him a slightly battered S4R Monster with its fuel-injected 113bhp 996cc race-derived motor and Roger promptly

took it home, stripped it down and threw away everything bar the motor, electrics, fork legs and brake calipers.

That's right – this is a true one-off motorcycle. There are no aftermarket parts on it whatsoever – even the brake and clutch lines from Venhill were one-offs. If you ❍

T-Bob came about as a result of his deciding to stop playing at bike building and get into it seriously.

SPEC SHEET

ENGINE
2003 Ducati S4R 996cc Monster, modified air box, modified clutch cover, one-off stainless steel exhausts by Allmond Cycle Design, oil cooler removed, one-off radiator by Pace Products

FRAME
2005 one-off perimeter monoshock by Allmond Cycle Design (ACD), stainless steel footrests & hangers by ACD

SHARP END
One-off hand-machined wheel by ACD, one-off discs by ACD, Brembo disc with one-off stainless steel cover, Venhill braided stainless steel brake line, modified Brembo master-cylinders, one-off reservoirs by ACD, Ducati/Showa forks with R/H bracket removed, one-off billet yokes by ACD, one-off stainless risers/handlebars/grips/internal throttle/brake & clutch levers by ACD

BLUNT END:
One-off HE30 tube single-sided swingarm by ACD, modified H-D softail shock with billet alloy & stainless covers, one-off hand-machined eighteen wheel with 300/35x18" tyre by ACD, one-off stainless sprocket/disc by ACD, heavily-modified Brembo caliper, Brembo master-cylinder, one-off offset front sprocket by ACD

BODYWORK:
One-off hand-made steel fuel tank with inset alloy console & Ducati clocks by ACD, one-off hand-made alloy seat unit by ACD

SPEC SHEET

PAINT

Ducati Red & black & white, prepped by Leo Crook, painted by Andy Peck

POLISHING

Everything that's stainless or alloy by ACD

ENGINEERING

'Bars, levers, grips, risers, yokes, fork covers, headlights, wheels & hubs, brake discs, sprockets, chassis, tank, fuel cap, switch covers, console, exhausts, 'pegs & controls, rad cover, timing belt covers, swingarm, shock covers, seat, rear caliper, & most of the nuts & bolts were hand-made & polished by Roger Allmond at Allmond Cycle Design

THANKS TO

'Luke Plummer & Ducati UK; All American Wheel for the wheel blanks; Avon Tyres; Andy Peck & Leo Crook for the paint; Earls Products; Pace Products; Venhill; Shell Oils UK; XYZ Machine Tools; Pat; & Pam Jones ...'

SPECIAL THANKS TO

'Emily, my wife, for putting up with me & it for all this time!'

were going to be picky then you could say that Roger didn't actually make the tyres himself but, hell, just about everything else on the bike, from the front wheel to the rear, was handmade by the man himself. It took ten months of incredibly long days all told (the rear brake caliper took three days all on its own) - the problem was that Ducati engines are notoriously hard to do anything with because they're not really designed to be on view (even the S4R Monster's engine is derived from the racebike 996s which are covered in acres of aerodynamic plastic) and, apart from one or two bikes based around the older air-cooled lumps, he'd never really seen one that looked balanced or that he liked.

So he started with a clean sheet and decided to do something pretty with the chassis. Once the lines and shape were established the rest of the bike just fell into place (apart from the seat which, he says, took a while to see before he could make it) - he wanted to build something that looked as though the Ducati designers in Bologna had had a hand in: It had to be instantly recognisable as a Ducati. He says that he did wonder whilst building the bike if it was worth all of the hassle – he'd sold all of his toys to finance the house and workshop, and he hadn't really earnt any money for the past three years because everything he'd done had been geared towards building a bike that was as good as anyone else

> **He wanted to build something that looked as though the Ducati designers in Bologna had had a hand in: It had to be instantly recognisable as a Ducati.**

in the world was building.

The fact that he's a complete perfectionist didn't help him much either, although you've got to be to build to this standard. He spent a week solid making some 'pipes, but ending up junking them because they just weren't right for the bike. That, he says, got him down a bit but, since taking it to the World Championships in Las Vegas at the end of last year and gauging the reaction over there from the press, public and other builders, he realises that he'd done the right thing. He wanted to go in at a level that would enable him to compete with the big names in the States and that's exactly what he's done. Although the bike didn't win its class he made some fantastic contacts

and had four or five big US magazines take photos of T-Bob (short for 'Techno-Bobber') to feature it.

His work has paid off over here too. As well as making the cover and centrespread of this august organ, T-Bob has also scored Roger a place on the Biker Build-Off UK. Discovery Channel sent a film crew along to the studio shoot to interview him and Victory Motorcycles donated one of their big vee-twin bruiser cruisers for him to work his magic over. Roger admits that it was a hell of a job to build something to this standard in just three months, especially as he works on his own, but he'd done a deal with the XYZ Machine Tools for a CNC mill and lathe so that should make things at least a little easier. ✪

WORDS: NIK
PIX: JOHN BRANDWOOD & NIK
MODEL: ANN FRENCH

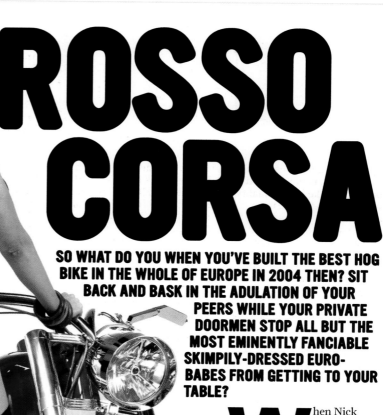

ROSSO CORSA

SO WHAT DO YOU WHEN YOU'VE BUILT THE BEST HOG BIKE IN THE WHOLE OF EUROPE IN 2004 THEN? SIT BACK AND BASK IN THE ADULATION OF YOUR PEERS WHILE YOUR PRIVATE DOORMEN STOP ALL BUT THE MOST EMINENTLY FANCIABLE SKIMPILY-DRESSED EURO-BABES FROM GETTING TO YOUR TABLE?

When Nick Gale's last bike, Memphis Belle, took the top honours at the European HOG event back in the summer of 2004, he was more than a little bit stunned. Yes, 'Belle was a lovely bike, he knew that, but he was up against some serious competition from all over the European Union and beyond and he wasn't expecting it to do that well. He'd been planning to set up in business building custom bikes for a while and the huge hit of publicity that he got from winning the top award meant that right then was a good time to set up Nick Gale Custom

> **He hadn't gone up there intending to buy anything in particular but, once he'd spotted the enormous thirteen inch wide Weld Recluse wheel with its 360 section tyre on display, he knew he just had to have one.**

Cycles ... so that's what he did.

Of course, having started out with a bike of that quality meant that he'd have to go some to top it. That's the trouble with going in big at the beginning – whatever you do next HAS to be even better or people start to think that you're a one-hit-wonder. He had a few ideas knocking about, but it wasn't until he went to the International Bike Show at the NEC in November 2004 that the germ of the seed for this bike was planted. He hadn't gone up there intending to buy anything in particular but, once he'd spotted the enormous thirteen inch wide Weld Recluse wheel with its 360 section tyre on display, he knew he just had to have one. He went and did the deal an

was just wandering back to his pick-up when his mobile 'phone rang. It was his dear old mum asking if he'd bought anything while he was up there and when he, without thinking too much about it, told her that he'd bought a wheel 'like the ones on the back of Formula One cars', the idea for the bike crashed into his consciousness with an impact similar to that of a six foot length of four b' two timber. He's always had a thing for themed bikes and that throwaway comment was enough to get the ball rolling – the new bike was going to be Formula One-themed. And, moving logically along, if it was going to be the best it could be, then that theme would have to be based around

the top team in Formula One ... yep, you guessed it, Ferrari. And, if it was going to be a Ferrari-themed bike, it'd have to be red and it'd have to have something to do with Michael Schumaker on it too because he's the Number One driver with them, isn't he?

Unusually these days, our Nick decided that he wasn't going to use one of the many variations on the Harley-Davidson vee-twin engine. He's a big fan of the Milwaukee Mo'Co's products and wanted a genuine Harley-Davidson engine in his bike, not one of its big inch impersonators, so he opted to base his bike around a proper H-D 1340 Evolution ◗

SPEC SHEET

ENGINE
2005 Harley-Davidson 1340 Evolution, polished S&S Super E carb, Wimmer twin stack air-filter, Barnett clutch, BDL primary with painted belt, Zodiac five speed gearbox, one-off exhausts by P&D Customs, Crane ignition, Goodridge braided stainess steel oil lines

FRAME
One-off by Cobra Engineering with elliptical swingarm & no centre post, Pro One forward controls, one-off centre stand by P&D Customs

SHARP END
23" Weld Recluse wheel, Weld Recluse disc, PM four piston caliper, Goodridge braided stainless steel brake line, two inch overstock SJP forks, SJP yokes, one-off 'bars by P&D Customs

BLUNT END
One-off swingarm by Cobra Engineering, Legend Air-Ride adjustable height rear shock absorber with on-board compressor, Weld Recluse 18x13" wheel, 360 tyre, Weld Recluse disc & pulley, PM six piston caliper

SPEC SHEET

BODYWORK

One-off front mudguard by P&D Customs, stretched Zodiac fuel tank with inset control panel with switchgear & Dakota digital instrument cluster by Nick Gale Custom Cycles, one-off seat by P&D Customs & Nick Gale Custom Cycles

ELECTRICS

Ness seven inch headlight, Kellerman 'bar-end indicators, Paul Yaffe radiused tail/numberplate light

PAINT

Rosso Red & airbrushing by Piers Dowell (www.piersdowell.com)

POLISHING

PT's Polishing

THANKS TO

'John Parry at Cobra; Dave Batchelor at P&D; Roger at Fullbore Motorcycles; Piers Dowell; & PT's Polishing ...'

powerplant. He took a brand spankers new motor that'd he done a deal on - along with a Zodiac five speed gearbox with BDL open primary and painted belt, his front and back wheels, and a set of two inch overstock SJP forks - down to John Parry at Cobra Engineering and, with a pretty solid design brief, commissioned them to come up with the one-off centre post-less steel trellis that you see before you. Cobra also made up the elliptical swingarm that cradles the massive rear wheel and is, in turn, operated by a Legend Air-Ride adjustable ride-height air shock that allows the bike to run with sensible ground-clearance, but be dropped down to sit with its belly nearly on the floor when parked. The more eagle-eyed amongst you may have noticed that the bike, named 'Rosso Corsa' after the famous red Ferrari colour scheme ('Rosso Corsa' translates as 'race red' and wasn't strictly a Ferrari colour – it was originally the national colour of all Italian racing cars be they Ferraris, Lamborghinis, Fiats or Abarths), doesn't actually have a side or centre stand in the conventional sense – it has a little stand that sits underneath which the bike lowers down onto when Nick drops the suspension down onto it. Clever, eh? The on-board compressor that powers the shock is neatly hidden away, along with the battery and all the electrical components, in the little compartment under the seat.

One of the main questions that he gets asked time after time after time is whether the exhausts burn his bum while he's riding? The answer is, of course, no ... it'd hardly be rideable if it set fire to your jacksie every time you took it out, would it? The majority of the heat is displaced through the front of the 'pipes and the rear sections are almost cold even when the motor's been running for a while (note the 'almost', don't go up and grab the 'pipes if you see the bike out and about, will you?). It is bastard-loud, though - it sets off car alarms almost at tick-

over ... as all the people with alarms on their cars in about a five hundred yard radius of the studio will no doubt now be aware after Nick started it up after the photoshoot. The other question he gets asked, though, always gets a resounding 'yes' as an answer – does the lack of back mudguard mean that he gets covered in road shite as soon as the roads get even slightly damp? Sometimes you just have to suffer for your art ...

And speaking of art (smooth link, eh?), the elegant Rosso Red, the Ferrari decals and amazingly life-like portraits of the German race-meister himself are all the work of a gentleman by the name of Piers Dowell. He's been responsible for some of the most beautifully intricate and over-the-top paint schemes around and specialises in almost photographic reality portraits ... as you can see from the pics hereabouts.

One of the main questions that he gets asked time after time after time is whether the exhausts burn his bum while he's riding?

He's now achieved his dream of having his own bike shop - Nick Gale Custom Cycles now operates out of a purpose-built showroom and workshop half a mile down the road from the Ace Café in London. The shop's address is Unit 5, Montague Works, 250 Water Rd, Wembley, London, HAO 1HX (020 8998 6775) and you can see all the stuff they do by surfing your way across to: *www.nickgalecustoms.co.uk* ✪

THE DELIQUENT

WORDS: **NIK** PIX: **JOHN BRANDWOOD** MODEL: **IRYNA**

SO, THE BIG QUESTION – WHAT EXACTLY IS A STREETFIGHTER? WELL, IT DEPENDS ON WHO YOU TALK TO.

At its purest, the definition of a streetfighter is a performance-based motorcycle that's been stripped of all unnecessary fixtures and fittings, tuned to produce as much rear wheel horsepower as is humanly possible and then painted/polished/ chromed until it looks far more aesthetically pleasing than it did when it left the manufacturer's showroom.

While most people with enough brain cells to rub together to produce a spark will agree with this, most of them will also be under the impression that the street-

This animal of an engine sits in a completely unmodified 1951 Speed Twin frame that's just been lovingly restored and detailed, and fitted with a host of period parts and accessories.

fighting motorcycle as we know it today has its roots in the early years of the Nineteen Nineties – something that isn't strictly true.

Y'see, people have been building performance-based motorcycles of this kind pretty much since the year Dot. Back in the Fifties in the USA, this was the thinking (well, apart from the pain/polish/chrome thing possibly) led to the creation of the chopper in its earliest form (where folk 'chopped' off everything that wasn't needed to actually make the bike work in an effort to keep up with the lighter and faster imported British machines) and, here, in the UK it was to lead to the

invention of the café racer. But, even before the clip-on 'barred café racer made its street-racing debut, people had been building hopped-up bikes with tuning parts a-plenty to go out and terrorise the British roads on – bikes that would've looked a lot like this little Triumph in front of you.

Okay, so Dick (and Del) from Baron's Speed Shop in south London's version of the 1950s hot-rod hooligan tool might be a hell of a lot more shiny than the bikes that'd've growled around the lanes of the Capital fifty years ago, but its heart is definitely in the right place. It takes all its styling cues from the more reprehensible end of biking's halcyon days and its motor? Well, you couldn't get any more hopped-up I can tell you ...

Starting at the top end, the 1951 Speed Twin engine has been fitted with a 1969 nine-stud splayed head that's been ported and fitted with Rowe Black Diamond competition valves and guides and heavy-duty springs with titanium collars. The original 500 barrels have been replaced with ▶

SPEC SHEET

ENGINE:

1951 Triumph Speed Twin, 1969 nine-stud splayed head, ported & fitted with Rowe Black Diamond competition valves & guides, packed R&D springs with titanium collars, Sonny Routt 750 big bore kit, honed an extra .002", 11:1 compression pistons, Harmon & Collins 7229 drag cams, twin Amal 389 Monobloc 1&3/16" bore carbs, Amal short chrome open bell-mouth filters, lightened/polished/balanced 1968 Triumph one-piece crank, Carrillo H-section steel rods, stock Triumph clutch run dry, Barnett plates, Devimead alloy pressure plate, stock Triumph primary drive, Reynolds Simplex 1/2"x 5/16" primary chain, stock 1951 Triumph gearbox, needle roller bearings on layshaft, 1970 close ratio gear cluster, Lucas competition magneto, modified stock 1&3/4" header 'pipes cut down to 3/4-1/2 to catch the pulse, about 60bhp from end of crank on 101 Octane leaded pump fuel (available from Park End Garage, Hither Green Lane, Lee, London SE12)

FRAME:

1951 Triumph Speed Twin, stock, stock footrests & hangers, Baron's Speed Shop footrest & gear-pedal rubbers

SHARP END:

Chromed WM1x21" rim, 1955-56 Triumph T100/T110 eight inch drum/hub (chromed), Avon Speedmaster 300x21" tyre, stock 1951 Triumph forks (chromed), Baron's Speed Shop replica Bates fork covers, stock 1951 Triumph yokes (chromed), stock brake cables, vintage Flanders handlebars

a Sonny Routt 750 big bore kit (that's been honed an extra .002") and 11:1 compression pistons, and the stock cams swapped for a set of Harmon & Collins 7229 drag cams. The carbs are a pair of Amal 389 Monobloc 1&3/16" bore items with short chrome open bell-mouth filters, and the one-piece 1968 vintage crank has been lightened and polished and balanced and fitted with Carrillo H-section steel rods. The clutch is the stock Triumph clutch (running dry though) that's been fitted with Barnett plates and a Devimead alloy pressure plate, and while the motor uses the stock Triumph primary drive, the primary chain has been uprated to a Reynolds Simplex 1/2"x 5/16"primary chain. The power this produces runs through a stock (as in original, not unmodified) 1951 Triumph gearbox, with uprated needle roller bearings on the layshaft and a 1970 close ratio gear cluster, and sparks are created by a Lucas competition magneto, while the exhausts are modified stock 1.75 inch header 'pipes cut down to catch the pulse. If you're not entirely au fait with old Brit

bike engines that list might not mean a hell of a lot to you so let me out it this way – a stock Speed Twin made about 27bhp if it was lucky ... this one makes about 60bhp!

This animal of an engine sits in a completely unmodified 1951 Speed Twin frame that's just been lovingly restored and detailed, and fitted with a host of period parts and accessories. The forks, for example, are stock '51 items that've been dressed up with a set of Baron's replica Bates fork covers and set in chromed yokes topped by vintage Falnders handlebars, while their other end is attached to a 1955/'56 eight inch hub/drum brake (chromed, of course) laced to a very skinny twenty one inch rim with a 3.00x21 Avon Speedmaster tyre. Mind you, the back tyre's not that much fatter either being just a four by eighteen on another chromed skinny rim laced, this time, to the stock Speed Twin fixed hub, but it looks right. They didn't have big chunky wheels in those days and 'The Deliquent', as the lads at Baron's have named it, would've looked pretty bloody stupid with something out of proportion crammed between its rear rails, wouldn't it?

Baron's scoured the shelves of their workshop and every supplier of NOS parts they

wotsit that looks like a vintage rubber battery case is a neat storage facility for tools, plugs and jets for when Dick wants to run the motor on methanol ...

While Baron's did the lion's share of the work on the bike themselves, when it came to the paint they felt they needed just a little help. They'd already laid on the lovely mini-flake aquamarine base coat and were dead happy with it but, they felt, a bike like this needed something a little extra. Neil Melliard is one of the best pin-stripers and sign-writers currently plying his trade in the hot-rod world and so he was contracted to come and wave his brushes over the tank and rear muddie - which he did so to perfection, as you can see.

That was it – 'The Delinquent' was done. Dick reports that it's an absolute animal to ride on the streets of his native London and it's put Baron's Speed Shop firmly on the customising map. They're currently building another Sixties streetfighter around a big bore '65 Bonneville and, get this, a bobber for none other than Ewan McGregor himself. On top of that they've started work on a Triumph streamliner that they're hoping to take to the Bonneville Salt Flats in the USA in 2007 to have a crack at record breaking; 'It might or might not be achievable', says Dick, 'but we won't know till we get there. Fuck it, just getting there will be an achievement!'.

If 'The Delinquent' floats your boat and you'd like something similar or you fancy a set of their white grips and rubbers or their fork covers or owt, then have a look at their website at: *www.baronspeedshop.com* or call them direct on 020 8405 4179. ✪

could find and sourced a very rare original 1960s Wassel banana fuel tank and one of the same company's ribbed rear mudguards too, and also a little Bates solo seat that they re-covered in white leather to match their own footrest rubbers and grips and sat upon a set of three inch springs. The oil tank and battery box are stock '51 parts that've been chromed, and that neat little

Dick reports that it's an absolute animal to ride on the streets of his native London (especially when it's burning methanol!

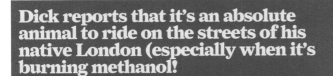

2010
Nov 25

ISSUE
136

OTHER BIKES FEATURED:
LPG BMW sidecar outfit, GSX11 chop, Dutch XS650

ODD JOB

A BOBBER? WITH KNOBBLIES? IS THE OWNER MAD? WELL, 'COURSE, AREN'T WE ALL?

WORDS: MR PK **PICS:** JOHN BRANDWOOD
MODEL: EMMA CLAIRE JONES (WWW.EMMACLAIREJONES.CO.UK)

Well, the story, I think it may have started after watching an episode of Biker Build Off. I mistakenly thought 'Yep, I can do that'. I soon became the owner of a 1988 883 Sportster in black with orange pin stripes and shiny bits - me and a mate collected the bike one evening from Gloucestershire. It wasn't an auspicious start - she broke down about half a mile from home.

Anyhow, I rode it around for a while to get used to the feel of the old bird. I've had a string of various sports bikes since passing my test back in 1991 so thought I should at least get the feel of the engine before I started pulling it apart. I soon got bored of it, though, and started sketching plans, and it must have been about that time, in 2004, that I first met Benny from Boneshaker Choppers at his old workshop in Tyseley, in Birmingham, not a million miles away from the old BSA works.

Well, Benny, being Benny, had his own plans for me and we never could agree - you see,

my plans involved sports bike parts and a sprung rear end and Benny's plans involved springers and a rigid frame, but we kept in touch quite regularly and I'd drop in and sit in the workshop and drink tea.

In the meantime in my garage-cum-workshop at home I attacked the Sportster with gusto. There was lots of angle grinding, welding and drilling into the small dark and cold hours of the night - the frame was chopped and the back end was binned, and the front end was re-raked and my latest eBay find was grafted on – an R1 upside-down fork ensemble with the bonus find of the decade: A one-off front wheel. On the back end I grafted a single-sided swingarm and big wheel/tyre combo, and it was rolling!

Skip forward a few years and

I was now divorced. Although I had a garage, most of my tools were in storage and the rolling bike was in basically the same state of build as the year previously. It was about this time that I decided that, on my own, it would take way too long to finish the bike. It was on one of my cup of tea visits that we were chatting again about what I was going to do with my rolling project. He still wasn't convinced of my crossover style, I could tell, but I agreed to give him fairly free reign on the project. I took over the engine and front end, with a load of other odds and ends, and told him to crack on. Over the following months there were numerous visits and chats about things. It was on one of the visits to the shop that Benny inadvertently came up with the name of the bike - he was ❯

My latest eBay find was grafted on – an R1 upside-down fork ensemble with the bonus find of the decade: A one-off front wheel.

SPEC SHEET

ORIGINAL YEAR, MAKE & MODEL:

1988 Harley-Davidson Sportster 883

ENGINE:

1988 Harley-Davidson Sportster 883, S&S Shorty carb with velocity stack, one-off 'pipes by Boneshaker Choppers

FRAME:

Fly-Rite Choppers Smokin' Gun, stock foot controls

SHARP END:

One-off custom wheel, Yamaha R1 brakes/usd forks/yokes/clip-ons, custom brake lines

BLUNT END:

16" Harley-Davidson wheel & brake

TINWARE:

Modified H-D Sportster tank by Boneshaker Choppers, cut-down fatbob rear mudguard, one-off battery & electrics box by Boneshaker Choppers, one-off oil tank by Boneshaker Choppers

2010
Nov 25

ISSUE
136

OTHER BIKES FEATURED:
LPG BMW sidecar outfit, GSX11 chop, Dutch XS650

> There were numerous visits and chats about things. Benny dug his heels in over some stuff and so did I but, generally, we were quite loose about stuff and it kinda just grew.

PAINT:

Rust worm & metal with artwork by Flakey Dave

POWDER COATING:

Frame via Boneshaker Choppers

POLISHING:

Boneshaker Choppers

ENGINEERING:

Spacers to fit R1 yokes to FRC frame/front hub to fit custom wheel to R1 forks & discs by Bhogal Senior at KC Engineering, all other work by Boneshaker Choppers

THANKS TO:

'The former Mrs PK for the divorce settlement without which it wouldn't have happened - sarcasm intended; Benny at Boneshaker Choppers for finally letting me talk him into it after much resistance; Bobby for the gearbox rebuild; KC Engineering in West Brom (0121 557 6663); Tilly, my seven year old daughter, just for being herself; & finally my dear friend, the late great Nick Tricket, who was always so excited about the project but never got to see it - I miss you mate.'

pleased with the way it was coming together and it was then that he thought it was 'ace even though it was a bit of an odd job'. That was it – the name just stuck.

Months passed and the day came to collect. It was late Summer 2009, warm and sunny, and as I rode away in the afternoon Sun I felt fairly happy with myself. It all turned out so well. I rode it to the pub where there was a BBQ on and lots of people gathered around it. It was to be a scene that continues to repeat itself everywhere I go on her - shops, motorway services, pubs, petrol stations, in the street, at traffic lights, the list goes on. Usually the first thing that tumbles out of everyone's agog mouth is, 'what is it?' ...

A while after collection, and a few hundred miles later, there were a few gearbox problems with the original 'box from the donor bike and so she came off the road in late Autumn 2009 and not long after she went into Winter hibernation until the salt was off the road in about April time. I was fairly stoked up about the coming year and when she came out of her den in the Spring it was

my intention to wind in some miles, and that's exactly what I have done. Every ride starts with a pre-flight check – it's amazing what can come loose when you have an 883 motor rigid-bolted to a rigid frame! Basically, everything needs to be checked and will need nipping up a quarter turn. One ride out to Bridgnorth for a cuppa with a mate turned into a full-on sprint to the Ponderosa Café at the Horseshoe Pass, but it was the ride back

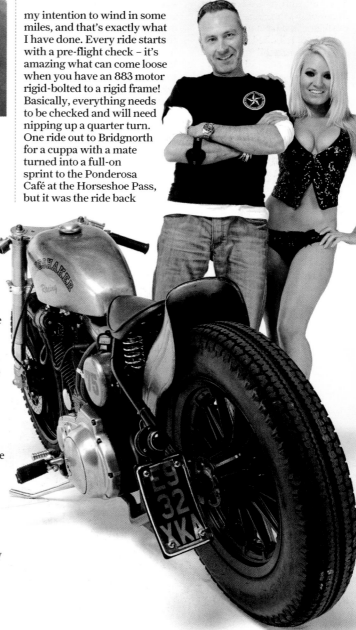

that got my attention when, banked into a corner, the road surface suddenly turned into a washboard. They're not very forgiving these hardtails!

On another ride things started to get a bit vibey - the counter-sunk cap-head bolts holding the sprotor (sprocket/disc) on weren't really holding it on any more, and the bracket that mounts the caliper to the frame had been totally destroyed. It looked like one of the bolts had failed, wound its way out and smashed into the bracket casting and most of the other bolts followed suit causing further damage. I was lucky to get away with

Every ride starts with a pre-flight check – it's amazing what can come loose when you have an 883 motor rigid-bolted to a rigid frame!

it just needing a few parts ...

Apart from that she's been a good girl ... except for shaking the rear 'guard almost to bits. That was another repair by Benny. Actually he's worked on the back 'guard twice – the other time was when, during a trip to Cornwall (yes, I know, I'm mad to go that far), I went over a quite a large bump at speed and the mounting bracket snapped clean off the frame ... although it could've had something to do with the barrel bag that was strapped to it. We must have looked quite a sight on the motorway with the mudguard rubbing on the tyre and creating a huge

rooster tail of burning tyre smoke. It was appropriately bodged at the services with bungee cords and the like, and the smouldering remains of shaved-off tyre rubber was peeled off the battery much to onlookers bemusement. There was a bit of a groove in the tyre, it's true, but I had to press on.

Actually, now I come to think of it, I've got lots of stories I could tell about our adventures, but I hate typing so that will have to do for now. Tally ho! ✘

SMALL BUT PERFECTLY FORMED

WORDS: NIK
PIX: JOHN BRANDWOOD
MODEL: TERRI DUGGAN

ANYONE WHO'S SPENT ANY TIME IN THE CUSTOM BIKE SCENE PROBABLY HAS A GOOD CHANCE OF HAVING MET HELENE, THE OWNER OF THE SMALL, BUT PERFECTLY FORMED, KAWASAKI TRIKE YOU SEE HERE IN FRONT OF YOU.

Helene and her other half, Budgie, have been building and smoking around on some very cool-looking bikes over the last few years – everything from big Jaguar-engined trikes to neat little hardtails through all points in between.

The motor in this, her latest trike, is from a crashed GTR1000 Kawasaki and was, pretty much, the only salvageable part. It sits in a rigid trike frame by the almost famous (well, in Dorset

anyway) Uncle Chufty and at the front the frame's attached to a set of billet yokes by Keith at PSP Engineering that hold a pair of motocross upside-down forks that've been mated to an aftermarket Harley rear wheel that's been turned into a front. The front brake disc is from the huge selection of stuff that Budgie has amassed over the years, and the front caliper is a little one from an RS50 Aprilia race-style moped. A moped also supplied the very neat tiny front brake and clutch master-cylinders that adorn the handlebars and they not only look the part, but work bloomin' well too.

Speaking of handlebars, these ones are also by Unc' Chufty too and they're a bit special. They're inch and a quarter in diameter, reducing to seven eighths at the ends, and they hold the internal throttle and all the wiring and cabling an' such. The internal throttle itself is made from a Honda C90 one, cleverly modified by the man himself, and now works beautifully. The switchgear is all aftermarket Harley stuff from Tubbsie down the

road at Jeez Louise Motorcycle Design, as are the neat little digital speedo and the handlebar grips too.

Back on the frame, the stock GTR radiator was replaced with one from Hants & Dorset Radiators and, according to Helene, cost about the same as a stock one, but could be made to a smaller and neater size while still keeping its cooling power. The OEM oil cooler was also Donalded and has been replaced with a much smarter one from streetfighter ◗

SPEC SHEET

ENGINE
Kawasaki GTR1000, K&N-type air-filters, one-off exhaust by JT Tubes/ Bikers Yard Salvage/ Moore Speed Racing/X Generation/Uncle Chufty, Moore Speed Racing oil cooler, oil lines by Twizzle Customs, one-off radiator by Hants & Dorset Rads (01202 301277)

FRAME
One-off rigid trike frame by Uncle Chufty, modified Kawasaki Z1000 rearsets as foot controls

SHARP END
Aftermarket Harley-Davidson rear wheel modified to suit, unknown Harley disc, Aprilia RS50 caliper, one-off caliper bracket by Uncle Chufty, Goodridge brake lines, motocross USD forks, one-off yokes by PSP Engineering, one-off risers & handlebars by Uncle Chufty, one-off fork tops & steering stops by Diesel Pete, Peugeot Speedfight clutch & brake master-cylinders, aftermarket old-style H-D switchgear, aftermarket Harley-Davidson digital speedo, modified Honda C90 internal throttle, aftermarket Harley-Davidson grips

BLUNT END
Modified Reliant Robin axle/diff/halfshafts/hubs by Uncle Chufty, Vauxhall Nova discs, Volkswagen Golf GTi calipers, one-off 15x12J Weller wheels, Nissan master-cylinder with one-off reservoir by Uncle Chufty

TINWARE
Modified Harley-Davidson fatbob fuel tanks by Uncle Chufty, one-off dash, one-off seat base by Budgie, covered by Steve (Man at the Back), one-off battery/electrics box by Uncle Chufty

SPEC SHEET

ELECTRICS

One-off internal loom by Budgie, Bates headlight, one-off LED cluster taillights with stop/tail & indicators, front indicators in backs of mirrors, blue/white LED marker lights, aftermarket windscreen washer lights as number-plate lights

PAINT

Black with silver tribal ghosting by Skin at Airyarts (airy.arts@virgin.net)

POLISHING/PLATING

Forks & fork tops by Twizzle at Twizzle Customs

ENGINEERING

Most by Uncle Chufty, emergency extras by Diesel Pete, yokes by Keith at PSP Engineering (01425 471018)

THANKS TO

'Uncle Chufty for turning the picture in my head into reality; Budgie for building it; Beaky for the 38 hour build marathon to get it finished for the IOW & just being there to calm me down; Bob for electronics rescue at midnight; Skin for the paint; Steve for the seat that cossets my bum perfectly & cripples my other half; Pete at Bikers Yard Salvage for understanding 'urgent' at 6am; Tom the blaster; Chris for the powdercoating; Simon at X Generation; Moore Speed Racing; Tubbs at Jeez Louise Motorcycle Design; John at JT Tubes; Flash for fitting me in; Bruce for the woodruff keys; Andy Lamb for the vinyls; Diesel Pete; Twizzle; Keith at PSP; & Veggie Dave for riding on the wrong side of the road in Spain & trashing the bike in the first place...'

You also have to bear in mind I had a budget of bugger all - I wanted the trick internal throttle, but without the trick price tag.

specialists Moore Speed Racing, and Chufty tucked it away out of sight.

While we're in the area, you can't miss that exhaust, can you? She'd seen similar zorsts on chops over the years and wanted something equally swoopy to help fill the space between the engine and the front wheel. It's a real joint effort – the pipework was done by JT Tubes, the sleeve for the can section came from Moore Speed Racing and the packing and baffling was done by south coast 'pipe specialists X-Generation.

A pair of H-D three and a half gallon fatbobs was designated as suitable fuel receptacles, but not before they'd been viciously attacked by Chufty – the gaps in the front and rear were panelled in for a tidier look and new mounts were

made underneath to take the coils, and to attach them to the frame too. He also made up a new dash 'cos she didn't like the stock one, and it was finished off with one of those lovely slow-motion pop-up filler caps.

Budgie made up the seat base and Steve 'Man at the Back' attached and shaped the foam that covers it, before making the super-smooth cover. Helene reports that, for her, the seat is bliss – it supports her lady parts perfectly. Budgie reports that, for him, it's feckin' agony – it squashes his man parts in a manner not conducive to him ever having children again.

The rear wheels are the one part of the trike that they'd consider changing in the future. When you go for tyres this wide, they're 345/35/15s, your choice of

wheels to fit them on is fairly limited - getting a set of posh billet wheels to take the tyres would've eaten up most, if not all, of her available budget. Steel wheels would be the answer, but even fewer people make wheels this wide in steel. She got onto Weller Wheels and managed to get him to make her a pair of 15x12Js in steel. It's funny but, while the trike may look huge with them stuck there on the back, it's actually small enough to go into the back of a normal-sized Ford Transit – the wheels sit between the wheel arches and everything!

Between the two hoops sits a very modified Reliant rear axle that's been narrowed so much that there's not actually a hell of a lot of it left. The diff has been rebuilt and tidied up, and the hubs converted to take Vauxhall Nova discs and

Volkswagen Golf GTi calipers. LED marker lights sit on specially-made arms low down in front of the tyres, and more LEDs illuminate the curved number-plate that hugs the axle. The rear lights are one-off LED clusters built into steel pods that are, in turn, mounted onto steel tubes that mount onto the frame. All the wires from the back go through the frame with all the clever resistors and all that gubbins inline – a hell of a lot of work, but they do look good.

Skin at Airyart is the man responsible for the deep lustrous black paint with its ghosted tribal graphics, and the world-renown (and real-life Wookie) Twizzle put the forks and anything else that needed polishing onto his polishing machine, and Budgie wired the beastie up ('cos he understands the black art of electrickery) and that was

pretty much all there was to it.

It was all worth all the hard work – the Kwak took 'Best Bike Trike' and 'Best Engineering' on its maiden voyage, and it's added a few more pots to their already groaning sideboard since then too. Helene is more than chuffed with it and is more than happy to talk to anyone about it too ... as long as you don't ask her about the lack of mudguards anyway. Y'see, while mudguards are part of Construction & Use regulations, they're not part of the MoT test so, if you're brave, you could argue that you don't need them. Lots of people don't know this, though, and she's becoming really, really short-tempered at being asked the same question over and over again; 'That can't be legal, it's got no mudguards?' Actually, it's quite amusing for those

of us in the know to prime some poor unsuspecting soul to utter the magic words and then stand back and watch the fireworks – just make sure there's nothing heavy or sharp anywhere within reach if you do it, okay? ✪

PURE BIKE PORN

WHILE THERE ARE MANY FOLK OUT THERE WHO ARE HAPPY TO TAKE THE FAIRING OFF A SPORTSBIKE AND CALL IT A STREETFIGHTER, FOR THE TRUE TWO-WHEELED TARMAC TERRORIST THERE'S ONLY ONE WAY TO ACHIEVE THE PINNACLE OF STREETFIGHTING PERFECTION . . .

WORDS: NIK
PIX: CLINTON
MODEL: NELSA

And that's to reframe the motor of your choice using the products of the two most respected names in aftermarket frame buildings – the bros Harris from rural Hertford or Sweary Bob Stephenson at Spondon Engineering in Derby.

Peter Harris is the proud possessor of this particularly fine example of Sweary Bob's craftsmanship. He heard that this 'ere turbocharged Spondon GSX was coming up for grabs. He knew the guy, Pete Dawson, selling it very well and had seen the bike in various stages of build and, knowing that Mr Dawson is somewhat of a perfectionist, knew that he just had to have it. He hot-footed it up to Pete (Dawson)'s house in (occasionally) sunny Stoke-on-Trent. Deals were struck, palms were spat on (and hurriedly wiped on trouser legs when the other wasn't

looking) and our Pete set off back to northish London with the bike of his dreams.

That was in the Winter of 2005 so, understandably, he didn't really ride it that much in the first few months of ownership. No, mostly he just sat looking at it in his garage; unable to believe he'd got his hands on something quite so sexy. The first real voyage out

on it, though, proved that all wasn't quite right as the motor kept oiling up number one and four plugs and generally smoking like, as he puts it, 'my dear old dad'. Figuring that this was down to a lack of use over the last few years, he put a new set of valve stem seals in but, while they did help, it was still smoking more than he was happy with so he set

Pete had just got rid of his Mag 1 in favour of the Mag 4 when, through the grapevine, he heard that this 'ere turbocharged Spondon GSX was coming up for grabs.

about rectifying it ... or rather looking for someone who could rectify it for him. He makes no apologies for not pulling the engine apart himself – he's handy enough when it comes to messing with motors, but really didn't fancy delving into the internals of something quite so complicated as this. Finally someone on the Old Skool Suzuki website recommended a guy called Steve at 2KTT Racing in Corby who was both willing to take it on and also able to do the job properly. Pete went and had a word with him, saw that he wasn't bullshitting and so entrusted his precious motor to his care with instructions to strip it down and replace what was broken while he set about sourcing all sorts of new power-boosting goodies from the US.

It wasn't long, though, before Steve was on the 'phone with some bad news. He'd replaced the seals in the turbo (they're generally the

most likely candidate for a smoky turbo motor), but the Spondon was still doing a fair impression of a balcony of a terminal cancer ward. Pete sighed and told him to take the head off and, as he'd expected, he found a horror story there. Pete says; 'whoever did the original engine build needs committing and shouldn't be allowed to go near an engine ever EVER again'. The liners were, to say the least, shagged beyond repair and at some time the clutch had let go too, and the head had been starved of oil as well, killing the cams. It also had four millimetres of

end play in the output shaft ... basically, it was Donalded.

Now at this point it would've been easy for him to blame Pete Dawson for it but, as he says, he's not the sort of guy who sells pups. Anyway, no matter whose fault it was, the motor still needed rebuilding so it was either rebuild it or break it up and get a Puch Maxi.

Hmm, I can see why you rebuilt it, Pete – Puch Maxis just don't do as good burnouts.

There was nothing for it, but to crack on and get it up and running. Pete says that he saved himself a fortune buying parts in from the States. The motor ⟩

SPEC SHEET

ENGINE

Buell S1 White Lightning, gas-flowed Thunderstorm heads, big valves, titanium collars, Mad Dog Racing rollers, Screamin' Eagle valve springs, Wiseco 1310cc big bore kit, one-off twin choke carb with one-off trumpets, strengthened crank, Barnet heavy-duty clutch, Baker six speed gearbox, Compufire ignition, one-off straight-through exhaust by Zorstec, Wizards of NOS' 40bhp single-stage nitrous oxide-injection kit, Nasty Bikes belt pulley, one-off outrigger plate by owner & Dockside Superbikes

FRAME

Buell S1 White Lightning, widened to fit swingarm by Dockside Superbikes, one-off polished sub frame by Dockside Superbikes, modified Vortex Yamaha R6 rearsets

SHARP END

Sixteen inch Revtech Aerofoil wheel, one-off Braking Wave discs, Harrison Billet Honda RC30-spec six pot calipers, one-off caliper hangers, re-worked & gold-nitrided black anodised WP usd forks, one-off wider billet yokes by Dockside Superbikes, one-off 'bars by GCS, Zodiac race controls, one-off master-cylinder reservoirs by owner, one-off switchgear by owner, Moto Gadget digital rev-counter & speedo

now boasts a specification that'd make a fair number of drag racers envious and puts out a barking mad 250bhp at only nine pounds of boost with a torque curve flatter than a railway line. The first time they put it on the dyno to set it up and it lit the tyre up as soon as the throttle was nailed. It drinks fuel like there's no energy crisis and sounds like a WWII Spitfire on full chat, and Pete says that, hand on heart, it's the most terrifyingly addictive thing he's ever ridden – when the turbo kicks

in, the front wheel comes up. That's it, end of story - no matter how fast you're going so you'd better be ready, okay?

Thankfully the heart of this psychotic animal is cradled in a chassis that's more than up to restraining it. The drop-dead sexy frame that surrounds it is one of only eight that Spondon built to take a turbo GSX motor and is aptly called a 'Monster'. Built from 43mm diameter alloy tube, it's just so goddamn horny-looking that you'd almost forgive it if it didn't work in much the

same way as you would a girlie who looked and dressed like Dita von Teese but couldn't cook. Attached to it at either end are a pair of wheels from a GSX-R 750WP – the front has Spondon fully-floating 320mm discs and Spondon calipers to haul it down from speed, while the rear uses a stock WP disc and a Brembo caliper. Forks (and yokes) are 1100 GSX-R items that've been rebuilt to the bike's spec by suspension gurus Maxton Engineering, and they're topped by Renthal 'bars in one-off billet risers with a World Superbike spec Brembo master-cylinder and a modified GSX-R quick-action throttle.

The swingarm is another of Bob and the crew's works of art in alloy tube and a top-spec Ohlins shock controls its movement. Up above it is a mucho-modified (and barely recognisable) RGV250 tailpiece and one-off seat, while the tank is another piece of automotive sculpture in alloy but, this time, it's the work of the world famous Tank Shop up there in Dumfries. It incorporates a built-in boost gauge, a quick-release filler and a high-flow fuel tap, and helps to give the bike that big-shouldered, almost bulldog-like look that all the best 'fighters have. Conventional

He makes no apologies for not pulling the engine apart himself – he's handy enough when it comes to messing with motors, but really didn't fancy delving into the internals of something quite so complicated as this.

GSX-R clocks sit in a one-off carbon surround inside the top of that maddeningly expensive headlight fairing that was made from a genuine Simpson RX8 helmet. The headlights now nestle behind the visor that Pete lifts to let the lights shine out when he's on it at night.

Paul at PDF is the main responsible for the paint and a damn nice job he's made of it too. One of my personal main criticisms of most Spondons is the owners never give them a lairy enough paint scheme, preferring to blow them over in plain colours. Spondons are NOT subtle bikes – they're about as subtle as being hoofed in the 'nads with a pointy shoe – so they need a paint scheme that compliments the in-yer-face-ness of the big tube frame but, and here's the trick, without overshadowing it. Paul's design is an almost perfect balance – it shows even the most fuckwitted of observers that this bike is something special, but doesn't distract from the engineering at the same time. Nice job, Paul.

Since it was finished, Pete's been out on it ... a lot. This is no trailer queen – he rides it. On the day of the shoot it was pissing down with rain, and accidents had delayed him from getting there on time, and we really weren't expecting to see him ride the Spondon up to the doors of the studio. He'd come down from his native Luton in weather so bad you wouldn't put a rat out in it on a bike that lights the tyre up on dry roads and was grinning like a Cheshire Cat. ✪

SPEC SHEET

ENGINE

Buell S1 White Lightning, gas-flowed Thunderstorm heads, big valves, titanium collars, Mad Dog Racing rollers, Screamin' Eagle valve springs, Wiseco 1310cc big bore kit, one-off twin choke carb with one-off trumpets, strengthened crank, Barnet heavy-duty clutch, Baker six speed gearbox, Compufire ignition, one-off straight-through exhaust by Zorstec, Wizards of NOS' 40bhp single-stage nitrous oxide-injection kit, Nasty Bikes belt pulley, one-off outrigger plate by owner & Dockside Superbikes

FRAME

Buell S1 White Lightning, widened to fit swingarm by Dockside Superbikes, one-off polished sub frame by Dockside Superbikes, modified Vortex Yamaha R6 rearsets

SHARP END

Sixteen inch Revtech Aerofoil wheel, one-off Braking Wave discs, Harrison Billet Honda RC30-spec six pot calipers, one-off caliper hangers, re-worked & gold-nitrided black anodised WP usd forks, one-off wider billet yokes by Dockside Superbikes, one-off 'bars by GCS, Zodiac race controls, one-off master-cylinder reservoirs by owner, one-off switchgear by owner, Moto Gadget digital rev-counter & speedo

WORDS: LARRY HARRIS
PIX: CLINTON@
STUDIOTHREE.ORG
MODEL: SHELLEY MARTIN

MODERN CLASSIC

BACK IN 1996 WHILE RECOVERING FROM A BROKEN LEG AND LOOKING FOR SOMETHING TO DO, I RESCUED A RATHER NEGLECTED TRIUMPH T150V FROM A BACK GARDEN IN REDHILL IN SURREY WHERE IT'D BEEN LEFT AFTER IT'D BEEN WRITTEN OFF IN AN ACCIDENT.

SPEC SHEET

ENGINE

1974 Triumph Trident T150V, standard head, new RSM valves/seats/guides, Hyde 1000cc barrels, standard cams, Mikuni 28mm carbs, K&N filters, Hyde stroked crank, standard clutch, Tony Hayward belt primary drive, standard gearbox, Boyer Micro Digital ignition, one-off headers by Andy Wood, one-off silencers by John Brown at J&B Classics, Lockhart oil cooler & braided lines

FRAME

1959 BSA A10, new steering neck, modified engine mounts, modified Norvil footrests & hangers

SHARP END

Suzuki Bandit 1200 wheel/calipers/forks/yokes/master-cylinder/clocks, EBC wavy discs, Goodridge hoses, Renthal 'bars, unknown Honda switchgear, one-off headlight mount

BLUNT END

One-off swingarm by J&B Classics, Koni Dial-A-Ride shocks, modified Suzuki GSX-R 750 front wheel, EBC wavy disc, Suzuki GSX-R 750 caliper, Ducati Monster master-cylinder, one-off torque arm by J&B Classics, one-off rear sprocket by Beaky's

t was a bit of a sorry state to put it mildly – just about everything bar the engine was absolutely destroyed but, luckily, the engine had been removed and stored in a neighbour's shed.

I salvaged what I could and started stripping down the engine to clean it all up, and then began collecting goodies to rebuild it. First came a nice set of 28mm Mikuni cards, then a Tony Hayward belt drive and then, while kicking around Kempton Park auto jumble, I came across a huge Norman Hyde 1000cc kit. It was at a good price, but I didn't have enough money on me. I didn't want to let it go, though, 'cos the chances of getting another one at anywhere near that price were pretty slim so I stopped people I knew at the auto jumble and begged and borrowed from anyone and everyone and managed to scrape together the cash.

Three or four months passed and the engine was finished. I was quite pleased with it – it was a bit of a fire-breather. The 1974 lump ran a standard head with new RSM valves/seats/guides, Hyde 1000cc barrels and pistons, the standard cams, Mikuni 28mm carbs with K&N filters, a Hyde stroked crank, the standard clutch, a Tony Hayward belt primary drive, the standard gearbox, a Boyer Micro Digital ignition, and a one-off exhaust. Andy Wood from Shoreham made the exhaust pipes for me. There's also a Lockhart oil cooler and braided lines. Right, so I had my motor ... what do I do with it?

Ideas bounced all over the place until I decided I wanted a nice little flat tracker-style street bike and so I began collecting the parts I'd need to build one. Five or six years and three house moves later a nice collection of part had accumulating on the shelves – a BSA A10 frame and its side panels, tool box and oil tank, a set of Norvil footrest hangers and footrests, a Suzuki Bandit 1200 front end, a GSX-R 750 front wheel to go in the back, a pair of Koni Dial-A-Ride shocks, an export Trident tank, a BSA A65 headlight and a fair few other bits and pieces too.

With all the parts accumulated, I shipped them all off to J&B Classics just up the road in Redhill to try and get them all joined together. Well, time went by, ideas got changed, bits got swapped and, in all, eighteen months passed before it was starting to look like the mental picture of it I had in my head. The fact that it looks almost like a ❍

> **Ideas bounced all over the place until I decided I wanted a nice little flat tracker-style street bike and so I began collecting the parts I'd need to build one.**

SPEC SHEET

TINWARE

Modified Suzuki Bandit 1200 front mudguard, modified Triumph T150 Export tank (widened 3"), one-off seat by Earl, one-off steel tailpiece/rear 'guard by J&B Classics, BSA A10 tool box & oil tank

ELECTRICS

One-off loom by J&B Classics, BSA A65 headlight, unknown rear light from Kempton Park autojumble

PAINT

Orange & black & white pinstripe by Brian at J&B Classics

POWDER COATING

Frame, swingarm, fork sliders, headlamp mount by some knobheads who lost my side stand

POLISHING

Owner

ENGINEERING

Swing arm/frame mods/spacers/clock & headlamp bracket/ everything that needed mechanically fettling by John at J&B Classics

THANKS TO

'John & Brian Worsel at J&B Classics (01737 770068); & PDQ for sorting out the carburetion ...'

---

factory bike (bar the big discs, of course) is testament to the effort that John and Brian at J&B put into it.

The BSA frame, for example, had to be slightly modified to drop the engine in (it was designed for a twin originally, remember, so cramming a wider engine with another cylinder was going to take some work) and it also had to be fitted with a new headstock to take the Bandit front end. I know I could've used slab yokes to make things easier, but they wouldn't have looked right – they'd've looked too custom, if you know what I mean? I got the big discs from EBC for a fraction of what the pukka Braking ones would've cost, and the headlight/clock mount was inspired by the one that Triumph originally used on the Hurricane X75.

The tank has been widened by three inches so it fits over the A10 frame and sits nicely parallel over the engine, while the A10 side panels went straight on without any fuss ... as you'd expect them to, really. The seat unit was made up in cardboard first to get the right look, and then it was made in steel with a drop in seat that's a nightmare to bolt up, but is worth the hassle 'cos you can't see the fixings. Earl, a very talented Kiwi chap, made the seat itself after I had given him the frame, tank and seat unit, and he moulded the seat to roll from the tank over the frame rails to the tailpiece. Neat eh!

I wanted to fit as fat a rear wheel as possible without having to mess around with the crankcases or offset the motor and that meant that I couldn't use anything much bigger than about a 120 or 130 section tyre. The Bandit rear wheel that I'd been offered with the front was, of course, much too big and so I picked up a GSX-R 750 front wheel and J&B modified that to take the rear sprocket instead. That left me with the option of putting another 320mm disc on the other side so I took it – it looks a bit mad, but I like it and that's all that counts, isn't it? Of course, using this wheel meant that the old A10 swingarm was now useless so J&B made up a new one-off box section 'arm to contain it. The rear brake caliper is also from a GSX-R (it's a rear one too, rather than another front), and the hanger and torque arm are one-offs by J&B. Koni Dial-A-Ride shocks keep the wheel away from the sub frame, and a Ducati Monster

---

I wanted to fit as fat a rear wheel as possible without having to mess around with the crankcases or offset the motor

---

> **I keep trying to change gear with the brake lever and brake with the gear pedal and it gets a bit hairy on occasion.**

master-cylinder operates the back brake when you put your left foot on it ... I still haven't got used to that. All my previous bikes for many a year, including my old GPz750 Turbo chop 'Terminator' and my Z1300 trike, have been left-foot 'changers and, although I had Brit bikes back in my Chopper Club days, I still haven't got used to riding a right-foot gear change bike again - I keep trying to change gear with the brake lever and brake with the gear pedal and it gets a bit hairy on occasion. The colour was always going to be orange and black because ... well, they're the proper colours for a flat-tracker, aren't they? Brian, John's brother at J&B Classics, did a wonderful job of it, paying careful attention to the design of the tank and side panel decals that he also had made for me. I did all the polishing and the final assembly – it'd taken the best part of ten years to get the final product together, but I think it's worth it.

I had a few teething troubles but it is a Triumph after all! It's a great little bike and I'm well happy with it. It goes nicely and it sounds lovely (the silencer was made by John and gives it that beautiful triple whine). God knows how much it cost (I'm afraid to add it all up), but it's kept me out of mischief for a while. ✪

ARSE ABOUT FACE

WORDS: **STEVE BEACHILL**
PIX: **JOHN BRANDWOOD**
MODEL: **GEMMA HILES**

IT ALL STARTED IN SEPTEMBER 2005 WHEN I HAD A CHAT WITH A FEW GUYS AT A V-MAX RALLY IN HEREFORD ABOUT THE POSSIBILITY OF BUILDING A V-MAX QUAD AND THE ANSWERS I WAS GETTING WERE ALL NEGATIVE ONES – IT CAN'T BE DONE, IT'S NOT POSSIBLE ETC ETC.

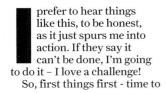

I prefer to hear things like this, to be honest, as it just spurs me into action. If they say it can't be done, I'm going to do it – I love a challenge!

So, first things first - time to find a donor bike. A 1988 full power model was purchased and used for a couple of weeks to check the suitability of the motor for the project. I was then told, though, by every insurance company in the country that they would not insure a quad ...

Plan B then, I would build a trike instead. I didn't want a conventional trike though as it'd been done so many times before. A trike builder in Newcastle relieved me of £3000 and returned it to me with less than 50% of the work done and to say I wasn't happy is an understatement. I was all ready to sack it off, but what saved the project from the scrap heap was one particular part - a special scaled-down handbrake built on to the frame brace that I'd commissioned Pegasus Engineering to build for me. It turned up in the post not long after the Baskerville event and spurred a whole new life into the project. Once I'd taken it out of its packing I thought I couldn't waste such a beautiful item - the craftsmanship that had gone into making it was exactly the way I had envisioned it. So back to the garage I went ...

I re-designed the steering set-up and a good local engineer built the new parts in just over a week and, once fitted, the steering was instantly more positive. The front actually utilises Ford Sierra hub mounts and hubs coupled to billet disc mounts that take the original V-Max discs and have a bracket to take the original 'Max calipers. Front brake lines were installed using Harley-Davidson clutch cable holders on the wishbones to keep the hoses from chaffing, and the mudguard brackets were originally made from 30mm flat bar, but I am having to redesign them as they flex too much and allow too much movement of the 'guards. ❍

SPEC SHEET

ENGINE

Buell S1 White Lightning, gas-flowed Thunderstorm heads, big valves, titanium collars, Mad Dog Racing rollers, Screamin' Eagle valve springs, Wiseco 1310cc big bore kit, one-off twin choke carb with one-off trumpets, strengthened crank, Barnet heavy-duty clutch, Baker six speed gearbox, Compufire ignition, one-off straight-through exhaust by Zorstec, Wizards of NOS' 40bhp single-stage nitrous oxide-injection kit, Nasty Bikes belt pulley, one-off outrigger plate by owner & Dockside Superbikes

FRAME

Buell S1 White Lightning, widened to fit swingarm by Dockside Superbikes, one-off polished sub frame by Dockside Superbikes, modified Vortex Yamaha R6 rearsets

SHARP END

Sixteen inch Revtech Aerofoil wheel, one-off Braking Wave discs, Harrison Billet Honda RC30-spec six pot calipers, one-off caliper hangers, re-worked & gold-nitrided black anodised WP usd forks, one-off wider billet yokes by Dockside Superbikes, one-off 'bars by GCS, Zodiac race controls, one-off master-cylinder reservoirs by owner, one-off switchgear by owner, Moto Gadget digital rev-counter & speedo

SPEC SHEET

ENGINE

Buell S1 White Lightning, gas-flowed Thunderstorm heads, big valves, titanium collars, Mad Dog Racing rollers, Screamin' Eagle valve springs, Wiseco 1310cc big bore kit, one-off twin choke carb with one-off trumpets, strengthened crank, Barnet heavy-duty clutch, Baker six speed gearbox, Compufire ignition, one-off straight-through exhaust by Zorstec, Wizards of NOS' 40bhp single-stage nitrous oxide-injection kit, Nasty Bikes belt pulley, one-off outrigger plate by owner & Dockside Superbikes

FRAME

Buell S1 White Lightning, widened to fit swingarm by Dockside Superbikes, one-off polished sub frame by Dockside Superbikes, modified Vortex Yamaha R6 rearsets

SHARP END

Sixteen inch Revtech Aerofoil wheel, one-off Braking Wave discs, Harrison Billet Honda RC30-spec six pot calipers, one-off caliper hangers, re-worked & gold-nitrided black anodised WP usd forks, one-off wider billet yokes by Dockside Superbikes, one-off 'bars by GCS, Zodiac race controls, one-off master-cylinder reservoirs by owner, one-off switchgear by owner, Moto Gadget digital rev-counter & speedo

I needed a bike for the rally so I pulled the trike apart and made a shopping list of parts that I needed to turn it back into a bike.

I pulled it out of the garage to test the steering and found that the standard rear wheel didn't suit the look of the project. I looked into wider rear wheels to suit the rear end, but the widest you could go with the standard swingarm was just a 180. I had a friend who had a Taylormade Performance Engineering swingarm/wheel on his bike and he sent me diagrams and dimensions of his swingarm and told me that it was done by using a second universal joint. Off to eBay I went again! I found a second hand U/J on the American eBay site and purchased it for the princely sum of £10 plus postage. While waiting for it to arrive I bought a pipe-bender off of a guy on the 100% Biker website to make my own swingarm.

The arrival of the second U/J meant that it was time

to get to work ... or was it? I'd forgotten that the two U/Js needed a stub axle to join them together. I sent a quick email to the friend I'd got the dimensions off and, luckily enough, he was stripping his bike for re-coating and had it all in bits. He lent me his stub axle and I duly sent it off to Pegasus Engineering who copied it exactly and also machined the casting off the U/J so that it would fit snugly in the carrier bearing. A set of lowered Progressive shocks was purchased from eBay for the princely sum of £30 and they set the back end nicely. A KR1S rear caliper on new brackets has

been fitted under the diff and a Willwood mechanical caliper, mounted on a bracket I made, on top of the diff to be used as the parking brake.

It was soon time to go for the dreaded MoT. It passed with only one advisory, 'sort those mudguard brackets, they're a bit flexy and will probably break after a bit of use'. Heeding his words I took it easy on the way back home and, lo and behold, 100 yards from my home the left hand mudguard bracket snapped, letting the mudguard spin 180

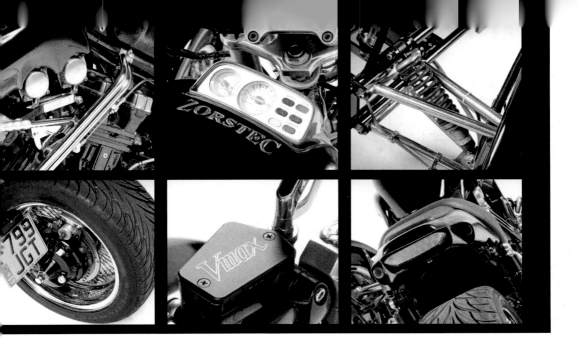

degrees on itself. Luckily the brackets that I had made were only temporary to get it through the MoT and I have since made more substantial ones to support the mudguards.

First time out on the road, the trike was a blast! The renovated motor was now making 122bhp (which is pretty good for a V-Max - don't believe all that 147bhp crap, that's an at-the-crank figure) and it was certainly no slouch. The new front end required a bit of fettling as it was a little bit light and required you to keep a loose grip, rather than a tight one, on the 'bars to keep it tracking straight and true, but I've since sorted that out and it's now fine. Sadly, though, I've had to sell the beast on and it's gone to live with its new owner down in South Wales. ✖

2009
Mar 19

ISSUE
114

OTHER BIKES FEATURED:
Honda chop, Kwak streetfighter, Rocket III

PURE

AS CUSTOM BIKES, AND THEIR BUILDERS, GET MORE AND MORE CREATIVE AND OUT THERE IT'S EASY TO FORGET WHAT THE WORDS 'CHOPPER' AND 'CHOPPING' A BIKE REALLY MEAN.

WORDS: NIK **PIX:** JOHN BRANDWOOD **MODEL:** BECKY JO HAYHURST

The clue is in the word – 'chopping' means cutting, as in cutting down, removing, simplifying, taking a bike right back to the basics of what it needs to actually be a motorcycle and no more than that.

These days the word 'chopper' has almost come to mean anything that doesn't look like a standard motorcycle and is instantly what the man in the street (or the woman, let it not be said that we here at Biker are sexist in our condemnation of woolly thinkers) gets a mental picture of when he (or she ...) hears the words 'custom bike'. Hip from So-Low Choppers in Stanton just outside Bury

St Edmunds in Suffolk is the builder (and, at the time of the photos, the owner too) of this very clean, very simple and, above all, very nice Dyna-engined chopper and, while he may not have intended to build what you might, if you were so inclined, call a retro-chopper, that's what he's ended up with. His actual rationale for constructing the

Choppers were, if you like, the first streetfighters – bikes purposely modified to be lighter, faster and, by definition, more in-yer-face than their stock brethren.

bike was to show that you can build, on a limited budget and in a limited timescale, a Dyna-engined bike that can hold its head up anywhere, and one which those who can spot something special will walk past endless rows of American Chopper look-alikes to go and look at. And if it turned out to be a good advert for his bike-building business too, well, that was a bonus, wasn't it?

He started the project with a 1340 Evo engine and the plan was to slot it into a classically simple rigid frame, made by his own fair (well, okay, oily) hand, with a skinny spoked front wheel and a set of springers up front, classic 'chopper' handlebars and a fat, but not stupidly so, spoked back wheel too. The tank and seat arrangement had to be equally simple and, while he knew he needed a rear mudguard, he didn't want some damn great cumbersome thing or, similarly, one the same as everyone else

has got on their bike. He also knew that, in the world of proper choppers, front mudguards are for poofs ...

So he set to, ably assisted by his young protégé Alec, his annoyingly talented fifteen year old son Jay and the electrical wizard (who, apparently, only wears his big hat with the sigils on when no one else is about) Mark. The Dyna engine was positioned in a jig, along with a rear wheel built around a stock Harley hub laced to a four and a half inch rim with

a 160/16 tyre on it, and a set of DNA straight-leg springers with a Mid West Motorcycles twenty one inch wheel and 90/90/21 tyre. Then, with the major components placed just so, he could then set about making up the clean and simple twin downtube rigid frame out of 1.25" CDS tubing.

With the frame done and ▶

SPEC SHEET

ENGINE:
Harley-Davidson Dyna 1340, Mikuni HSR 42 carb, Santee exhaust, points ignition, converted to chain drive

FRAME:
One-off rigid by So-Low Choppers, BDL forward controls

SHARP END:
Mid West wheel, polished stainless disc, Ultima caliper, DNA springers, Earl's brake line, z-bars, BDL master-cylinder, microswitches, MMB speedo

BLUNT END:
Stock H-D hub laced to 4.5" rim, polished stainless disc, Ultima caliper, BDL master-cylinder

TINWARE:
Sportster tank, Ultima seat, So-Low Choppers rear 'guard

2009
Mar 19

ISSUE
114

OTHER BIKES FEATURED:
Honda chop, Kwak streetfighter, Rocket III

ELECTRICS:
One-off loom by So-Low Choppers, Ultima headlight, Iron Cross rear light

PAINT:
Green metalflake by So-Low Choppers

POWDER COATING:
Frame & engine by Aerocoat (www.aerocoat. net or 01493 488455/6)

ENGINEERING:
Head steady, torque arm, frame etc by So-Low Choppers (www. solowchoppers.co.uk or 01359 253600)

THANKS TO:
'Mark, Alec & Jay at So-Low Choppers; Aerocoat for the usual excellent job on the powdercoat; & Mid West Motorcycles for parts...'

dusted a short while later, he could now start offering up other components to see how they looked. A Sportster tank was the only thing he thought would look right for the style of bike he was building and so one o' them was attached with deceptively simple mounts, and that very subtle rear mudguard, with its lovely unobtrusive curving struts, was made from a Mid West item and was widened and adapted to suit. An Ultima single seat, with a couple of small springs below it, was positioned exactly where it looked right, and he knew straightaway that the 'bars had to be Z-bars to give the look he wanted. The forwards are off-the-shelf BDL ones and, not wanting to be quite the same as everyone else, he forwent the usual Bates headlight in favour of a much more

shapely Ultima one. The rear light is, of course, an Iron Cross one – this is a proper chopper after all, remember.

With all the parts wot he wanted decided upon, the bare metal bike was then stripped and the frame and the bare engine sent off to the powdercoaters. The paint was next and it, again, was handled by Hip himself and he made a flawless job of the green 'flake on the tank and rear muddie.

Mark

knitted together a so-minimal-it's-almost-invisible loom that's so hidden it could give Osama bin Laden hiding lessons, and a set of Santee exhausts and a tiny MMB speedo were bolted on for the

MoT, purposes of. Just five short weeks after he'd started, Hip had a fully-finished, up-and-running custom motorcycle that he was more than a bit proud of and one that he fully intended, when the weather got a bit better, to get out and do some miles on. Well, that was the intention anyway, but no sooner had he rolled it from the work area into the showroom at the front of So-Low than Gilly from the Chopper Club came in through the front door, saw it and just had to have it. A deal was done, palms were spat on (and then hurriedly wiped on trouser legs when the other person looked away) and Gilly was the proud owner of one of the nicest, simplest chops I've seen in a good while. ⊗

2008
Mar 20

ISSUE
101

OTHER BIKES FEATURED:
1926 Rudge, Hongdou 200, Exile Harleys

EVEN THOUGH THIS IS NOW MY (NIK) BIKE, I THOUGHT IT'D BE A LOT MORE INTERESTING TO HAVE BAZZA, THE GUY WHO BUILT IT, TELL YOU ALL ABOUT IT.

WORDS: **BAZZA (& NIK)**
PIX: **CLINTON AT STUDIO THREE**
MODEL: **VANNESA UPTON**

THE
CHANGELING

Some things about the bike have changed over the years (like the exhausts), but it's still pretty much as he created it way back in 1989.

'Being a courier (and one who'd seen 'Mad Max' at that) showed me how to get as much from a bike as possible with minimal outlay and matt black and dirty doesn't necessarily mean badly maintained or dangerous.

One day a friend told me he'd seen a GS1000 that was sixty five percent complete for a paltry £300. After a couple of weeks of bodging, it seemed like a fairly good, solid bike but within a week it spat out number two sparkplug at my left leg. Then a few days later the tank fractured from forced contact with the frame, leaking all over my legs. I limped it home and tried to find a suitable tank among friends, and turned up a small genuine Harley Sportster tank for free from a pal.

With the Kent Show fast approaching, I had my work cut out. The tank looked good sitting on the top tube of my frame, but it just didn't look right with the standard seat or even the standard seat rails. Something had to be done.

I stripped it down to the bare minimum, fixing the frame into place with a spirit level, before shaping and tacking the new rails on as low as was possible. Once they were in position and checked for alignment, the standard rails were cut away, immediately giving the desired shape and contrast with the high tank. Once the seat was bent and fixed on, the frame and mudguard were trimmed severely short, the battery and electrics were squeezed under the seat, the wiring loom was cut back and trimmed of all excess, a Fizzy rear lamp fitted and the rear footrest hangers were chopped off and the 'pegs remounted in the triangular steel sheet side panels I'd made. I pulled the big wide handlebars off dead DR400 to replace the narrow standard bars and was hit by the idea of using its twin lights on a fairing stalk. It became the most discussed aspect of the bike and the most copied.

The last bits of chrome were covered with two sets of fork gaiters and a fresh coat of matt black was applied. I could hardly believe I had finished with only a couple of days 'til the weekend's show. It looked just right. All the lines flowed. Everything looked in the right position, proportion and ratio to each other - it definitely had a certain something, cheap and cheerful though it was. It was lean and mean, quite petite and ▶

> **After a couple of weeks of bodging and banging in the back garden, behind the off-licence that we lived above, it looked something like a bike and not a penny spent.**

very understated in one way and strangely imposing in another.

When the time came to replace the rear tyre of the GS, a mostly-worn Metzeler Sahara 130/17 was found for free and tried. It added to the bike's weirdness and worked great, so I had to get a matching front tyre. I got an early GS750 hub laced to a 17" rim, and fitted new 140 Sahara knobblies. I also made up a grab 'bar out of steam pipe for my girlfriend to hold onto, and some new 'pipes that ran back almost to the rear wheel spindle - one pipe down the left and three down the right side. They sounded awesome - more like an old WW1 fighter plane than a bike. The only thing bugging me was the odd wheels and every time a FatBoy came by, it got me to thinking - lust as I might over Fat Boy wheels, I was NEVER going to waste money and buy a pair. A certain type of dustbin lid - one that more than resembled Wandsworth council bins - was just the right dished shape and solid flexibility. I cut the inner and outer edges as best I could and held them together with four bolts and locknuts, covering up the not too perfect joins with black bathroom sealant. After taking the shine off with rough sandpaper and giving them the all important matt black, I was astounded at their effect.

> I stripped it down to the bare minimum, fixing the frame into place with a spirit level, before shaping and tacking the new rails on as low as was possible.

A Quickbob tank, mounted on a set of car exhaust rubbers, replaced the Sportster and gave better range (I've toured Europe on it a few times) and, when the GS1000 lump finally gave in, it was replaced with a hybrid ESD/EF1100 after carefully grinding all the Suzuki and TSCC badges from the castings.

The name, 'The Changeling', came from the words of the first track of The Doors' 'LA Woman' album as it was always moving, changing and evolving. That year at the Bulldog Bash, I was absolutely stoked to have Odgie approach me wanting to feature it and it went into his new and wonderful creation, AWoL (number 1 no less!).

After being beaten at the Bulldog Bash by a turbocharged bike, I decided that the next step could only be a turbo. I found one complete with an S&S Super B carb, oil feeds and boost gauge from a drag-racer in Swindon for only £600. I had never ridden anything like it before and never will again - it was totally stupid and virtually uncontrollable, wheelieing in EVERY gear. If I wasn't burning my left leg on the ridiculously short exhaust, then I was having my right leg sucked into the enormous carb bell-mouth, but I just got on as best I could with severely pissing off every Power Ranger I could find - it was so much fun seeing them trying to get away from the nasty scabby black thing that made so much noise, only to be overtaken by it, on one wheel. Happy days ...

There's a strange myth about how the next owner came into place, involving boats sunk by happy trippers and drunken scuba diving in the Thames - every bit is true!' ✖

WORDS: **IRISH PAUL**
PIX: **JOHN BRANDWOOD**
MODEL: **ANNIE NORRIS**

LIZZIE

ONE OF THE MANY QUESTIONS I GOT AT THE START OF BUILDING MY SUNBEAM SPECIAL WAS 'WHY?' OF COURSE MY RESPONSE WAS 'WHY NOT?'

SPEC SHEET

ENGINE

2004 Buell XB9R, converted to carb, Sporster 1200 carb, modified Sunbeam air-filter cover, custom air-filter, AMM-IMMOGNITION II single-fire ignition, Spyke coils, one-off stainless steel exhaust with stock Sunbeam silencer by Martyn

FRAME

1951 Sunbeam S8, strengthened backbone, engine used as stressed member, detachable lower rails, designed & done by Martyn

SHARP END

16x5" Harley-Davidson rim (powdercoated), modified Harley-Davidson rear brake hub, aftermarket Harley disc, Harley-Davidson Dyna rear caliper, modified Sunbeam S8 forks, Sunbeam S8 yokes, modified Sunbeam S8 'bars with 1" Harley-Davidson switchgear

BLUNT END

Modified BSA/Sunbeam plunger, 16x5" Harley-Davidson rim (powercoated), Harley-Davidson 883 Sportster rear pulley, modified Sturgis belt, modified Harley-Davidson rear brake

I'd been thinking about building a one-off special for a while - I knew I wanted something older than 1973 and with a big enough engine to take me anywhere I wanted to go.

Looking through my online parts store (eBay) I came across a 1951 Sunbeam S8 frame. It was twisted, but it was only a tenner! I always liked Sunbeams - I remember seeing my first one at the NW200 many years ago and when I saw the frame on eBay I knew that's what I wanted.

With the frame sitting on my basement workshop my thoughts now turned to what engine to use. Again the online parts store came trumps. I found a 2004 Buell XB9R engine going for just over 500 quid! I thought that as the frame would be the most important part of the build I would get an expert to make the mods to get the engine to fit. I thought this bit would be easy – there are plenty of engineering works about that specialise in bike mods, right? Wrong! Most of them said it could not or should not be done. I finally found a place but, long story short, they messed me about. I did however get to speak to one of the guys who was working on my bike. His name was Martyn Wakefield and he liked what I was trying to achieve and so when the engineering works laid him off I decided to get him to help me finish the bike. Now Martyn is old school - he's been riding bikes for most of his life and he can weld anything (and I mean anything) so, with my ideas on how I wanted the bike to look and his engineering knowledge, we were in an ideal

> **The only reason I could not see why it was not going for a higher price was maybe because it has different engine mounts to other Buells and Harleys, but that wasn't a problem in my case.**

place to get the bike done. Martyn and I spent many an evening discussing how to put the bits of the bike together and I do plan to write all the mods down and put them on a website but, for the moment, I'd like to highlight a few which Martyn and I are especially proud of.

As the frame was twisted the lower part had to be replaced. However, using the Buell engine as it was in the original bike – ie. as a stressed member – meant that the lower part of the Sunbeam frame could be made to be detachable. This makes it easier to remove the engine, but also allowed us to keep it nice and tight design wise. Cool idea or what!

The wheels and braking system are all Harley - the rims are exactly the same shape as Sunbeam ones (wonder if Harley copied Sunbeam?). I did look at using Sunbeam rims, but when I got a whole H-D wheel for ▶

2008
Apr 17

ISSUE
102

OTHER BIKES FEATURED:
1926 Rudge, Hongdou 200, Exile Harleys

The wheels and braking system are all Harley - the rims are exactly the same shape as Sunbeam ones (wonder if Harley copied Sunbeam?).

less than twenty quid so I couldn't argue. Again to keep with the look of the 'Beam I used old-fashioned style hubs, but with disc brakes front and rear. The forks have been reversed to allow the brake caliper to use the original brake hub mounting bracket and, from memory, the axle was only 1mm too thick for the H-D hub and only needed a simple mod to complete the mounting.

The engine has a carb from a 1200 Sportster jetted to suit and a fibreglass Sunbeam air cleaner cover with a custom filter inside, and the oil cooler is an old brass heat exchanger from a boat with a part of an exhaust with a bell end. I call it a 'Ye Oldie Ram Air System'! The exhaust is a one-off stainless steel system using an original Sunbeam silencer and, while it definitely looks the part, it's not quite finished (heat shields are still to be added).

I got most of the tinware from David at Stewart Engineering, the only place you can get Sunbeam S7/S8 parts. The battery box was converted into an oil tank as the Buell engine is a dry sump engine (the battery now sits behind the engine), and the electrics box was straightened and modified to suit the frame and now houses the coils and main electrics. The tool box and front and rear mudguards are all fibreglass and the front and rear mudguard brackets were modified to suit, and the petrol tank was stretched a

wee bit to keep the look of the bike (and it needed a fair bit of welding to fix all the holes!). The last thing, bodyworkwise, was the seat – it was converted from a S8 mounting to an S7 one to allow the cantilever set-up to be used.

The electrics are a complete one-off by myself, but what I think really stands out is the digital speedometer. It's a Dakota Digital HLY-3016 and it fits nicely into the original housing in the headlight. It also contains all the gauges in one unit (ie. oil, fuel, amp gauge, oil pressure, oil temp, indicators etc. etc) and this means it keeps the clean look of the original bike. The original amp gauge was replaced by an oil pressure gauge, and the ignition is controlled by an AMM Immognition II single fire ignition system which it totally programmable to suit the bike. I used a modern lighting system with LED rear brake/ stop light.

That really just left the paint and I did that myself plainly and simply using gloss black spray cans from Halfords – I didn't want it to be flash and shiny, I wanted it to look, until you looked closer, like a bike that'd been built in the 1950s. It seems to have worked – everywhere I go on it, it draws a crowd and one person even asked me if it was a Vincent Black Shadow ... ✪

SPEC SHEET

TINWARE
Fibreglass Sunbeam S8 replica front mudguard, modified Sunbeam S8 headlight cowl, stretched Sunbeam S8 fuel tank, modified Sunbeam S7/S8 seat, modified Sunbeam S8 battery box, Sunbeam S8 electrics box, fibreglass Sunbeam S8 replica tool box, fibreglass Sunbeam S8 rear mudguard

ELECTRICS
One-off loom by owner, Dakota Digital HLY-3016 digital speedometer, halogen headlight, LED rear light

PAINT
Black Halfords spray cans by Team Wot

POWDER COATING
Frame & beltguard by US Enamelling, Knaresborough & wheels by C.Wylde & Sons, Leeds

POLISHING
Todge (Steve Jordan)

ENGINEERING
All frame & tinware mods by Martyn Wakefield

THANKS TO
'Alison, Ben & Jacob, me family, for putting up with this project over the last three odd years; Martyn Wakefield for helping me with all my strange ideas; the Sunbeam Owners Fellowship (www.onthebeam. co.uk) for advice on Sunbeam stuff; David & Christine at Stewart Engineering; & finally my dad for being there ...'

2008
May 15

ISSUE
103

OTHER BIKES FEATURED:
Long-forked Triumph twin, Hinckley hardtail, Dutch BSA

SPIRIT OF THE SIXTIES

WORDS: **GARRY LAURENCE**
PIX: **CLINTON**
MODEL: **JO LAURENCE**

THIS BIKE WAS CONCEIVED SOME THIRTY FIVE YEARS AGO IN MY MATE'S FRONT ROOM, BEFORE THE ADVENT OF COMPUTERS AND LATE NIGHT DRINKERS, AND IS THE THIRD IN A SERIES OF SPECIALS.

There was not much to do when returning from the local bike café, Johnson's on the A2 by Brands Hatch, but sit around drink more tea and coffee and talk bikes. This is when all the planning of a bike we were never likely to build took place. They were never built because, even back then, these were expensive and we just never earned enough money to fulfil those ambitions.

At the time TriBSAs and Tritons were the order of the day and Norvins were a rare beast indeed, but they fired my imagination as the King of the Café Racers. As time went by I drifted away from bikes, eventually selling my eight valve Westlake Triton, and moved onto cars but I never lost the dream of building a Norvin.

My return to building specials and restoring standard bikes came about with the purchase of a Triton that had been laid up for years. I bought this from a work colleague and set about building a Triton to rival the best. I named this bike 'Spirit of the Sixties' and, having completed this and with appearances in the classic bike magazines, my attention was once again focused on building a Norvin.

I searched for a long time to find a suitable Vincent engine but everything I looked at was very expensive, used and abused, and worn out with broken fins and leaking oil everywhere. In the end I purchased a wreck of a 500cc Norvin that'd been in a back garden for years, threw ninety percent of it away and started from scratch. This was the basis for the next special, 'Spirit of the Sixties 2' which, again, graced classic bike magazines, but all the time I still had my sights on the ultimate prize - a 1000cc Norvin café racer built to a standard not seen before.

Having failed to find a suitable engine and getting hacked off with travelling hundreds of miles in search of the Holy Grail I decided the way forward was to build a new engine. A good friend of mine, John Wyatt who runs the Norvin Centre, did me a very good deal on all the major parts required to build the engine, and Gary Drake at the legendary Godden Engineering was given the task of actually building it into one piece. To fund this project I had to sell the Triton because today's prices for anything Vincent are worse than ever and I was not prepared to cut corners. While the engine was being built I concentrated on the rolling chassis - I purchased a ◗

SPEC SHEET

ENGINE

Vincent 1000cc air-cooled v-twin, built to Black Shadow specification by Gary Drake at Godden Engineering, twin plug heads, MK II cams, 32mm Amal carbs, velocity stacks, newly-machined Vincent flywheels, Vincent Black Lightning con-rods, V2 multi-plate semi-dry clutch, triplex primary drive, BTH twin spark self-energising electronic ignition, one-off alloy offset gearbox sprocket, twin 1&5/8" stainless steel Black Lightning-style exhausts, stainless steel oil lines, minimum of 55bhp@5700rpm

FRAME

1954 Manx Norton, modified foot rest hangers, Barleycorn Engineering foot rests & levers, top frame rail modified to allow valve cap removal, oil return line & timed breather pipes bronze welded to frame, rear frame spreader modified to take rear engine mounts & oil tank mounting platform, various brackets added for horns & wiring

"In the end I purchased a wreck of a 500cc Norvin that'd been in a back garden for years, threw ninety percent of it away and started from scratch."

2008
May 15

ISSUE
103

OTHER BIKES FEATURED:
Long-forked Triumph twin, Hinckley hardtail, Dutch BSA

SPEC SHEET

SHARP END

19" Morad stepped alloy rim, stainless spokes, Yamaha TZ350 10" four leading shoe brake with laser cut frames & stainless steel mesh for cooling, green racing brake liners, short Manx Norton Roadholder forks, stock Manx Norton bottom yoke, one-off alloy top yoke, one-off stainless steel swan-neck clip-ons designed by owner, standard Lucas switchgear, chronometric speedo & rev counter with synchronised needle sweeps, modified Norton Commando surrounds

BLUNT END

Manx Norton swingarm modified to take Norton-designed chain guard & speedo cable support brackets, Koni adjustable shocks, Reynolds chain, one-off alloy offset sprocket, 19" Morad stepped alloy rim, stainless spokes, Yamaha TZ350 brake hub modified to take speedo drive, green racing liners

TINWARE

Standard Manx Norton front mudguard mounted on home-made 'y'-shaped brackets, hand-made four gallon Manx-style fuel tank, Manx Norton-style alloy single seat with one-off cover designed by owner & made by Blackbird Leathers, Manx Norton rear mudguard modified with twin breather pipes for engine & oil tank, one-off alloy Manx Norton-style central 'elephant's foot' oil tank

Manx frame and V5, Manx forks, TZ Yamaha racing brakes, swan-neck clip-ons etc and, for a long while, that was it. Eventually I got a call from Gary to say I could pick the engine up. I placed it in the frame and pondered for some time as to whether to machine off the swinging arm lug cast into the rear of the cases that stops the engine from going into the frame neatly. This is deemed to be sacrilege on a Vincent engine by Vincent enthusiasts and, being a Vincent owner myself, I can understand that point of view. This, however, is not a 1949 HRD engine or of historical interest – so off came the lug. I then made the engine plates to suit. The only problem, other than having to make several sets of engine plates before I was satisfied with the fit, was that I had to alter the top frame rail to allow the removal of the valve caps to do the tappets once the engine is installed - this was simply a matter of cutting a crescent moon shape out of the frame rail and bronze welding it back in reversed.

With the engine in I took the rolling chassis to my local tank man for petrol and oil tanks, the chain guard and the seat to be made. Steve, the tank man, insists on making custom fit tanks to each individual frame because he then knows they will definitely fit - this guy is an artisan in working aluminium and produces the best work available and, although you have to wait, it's worth it. He cursed me more than once as I would not compromise on design and he had to make the Manx 'elephant's foot' oil tank so I could fit it from the rear and this meant the rear wheel, swing arm, rear frame spreader and mudguard had to be removed to allow fitment.

With the tanks made it was the exhausts next - the last piece of the dry build. I used John at Campbell Custom Exhausts as he had made the two inch straight through 'pipe for my 500 Norvin. I designed the 'pipes using foam plumbing pipe lagging taped into position and John made the 'pipes to this design, not conventional but it worked.

With the dry build complete and all brackets made and welded into position it was time to strip it down for paint and powder coating. Phil at Bikecraft, who does all my painting, was given a brief of what I wanted and has produced a show-winning paint job, and the seat went to Gary at Blackbird Leathers for the seat cover to be made and embroidered with the name of the bike, 'Spirit of the Sixties 3'.

The day came to fire the beast up. The engine, being all new, was very tight and did not spin over easily but, after ten minutes or so, it fired and ran very well. All systems were checked out and I booked it in for the MoT. On arrival at the station I kept the bike on low revs bearing in mind the straight through 'pipes - they raised an eye brow or two, but all was well when I explained they built them like this in the Fifties ... With MoT and insurance it was off to the Post Office for my free road tax. After some debate as to whether it was free or not, they conceded and gave me the road tax as the original bike hadn't been taxed for donkeys' years.

What's it like to ride? Just superb! After thirty five years of waiting it's all that I expected and more. It handles and brakes like it's on rails, and the power is awesome. The noise from the exhausts is a touch anti-social – it sounds like a dragster on steroids. Was it worth it? You need to be the judge of that - my view is that 1500 hours of work and a serious pocket lightening have produced the motorcycle of a lifetime. You bet it's worth it! It stops

traffic and brings a smile to my face every time I ride it. People wait around just to hear it start. It even makes some kids cry and their mothers frown ... I can't imagine why. One guy summed it up for me, 'that's automotive pornography, mate'. ✪

> ## "You bet it's worth it! It stops traffic and brings a smile to my face every time I ride it."

SPEC SHEET

ELECTRICS

Main loom designed & made by owner, Alton alternator, Boyer Powerbox for direct lighting, no battery, 7" Lucas headlight, standard Lucas tail-light with water jet-cut Vincent emblem

PAINT

Silver with black & red coach lines, airbrushed Norton/Vincent tank logo, mudguards in two pack black by Phil at Bikecraft, Kent

POWDER COATING

Frame & swinging arm by Morden Powder Coating

POLISHING

All aluminium polished by owner, every stainless nut & bolt hand polished

ENGINEERING

Engine built from new parts supplied by John Wyatt at The Norvin Centre & built by Gary Drake at Godden Engineering, foot pegs & swan-neck clip-ons by Barleycorn Engineering, tanks & seat made by local firm, all other parts designed & made by owner

THANKS TO

'John Wyatt at The Norvin Centre (01708 470526); Gary Drake at Godden Engineering (01372 844072); Phil at Bikecraft (01258 0765578); John Campbell at Campbell Custom Exhausts (07946 759990); Gary at Blackbird Leathers for the seat cover (0208 460 0373); Barleycorn Engineering (01379 586728); & Jo for modelling with the bike ...'

2009
Feb 19

ISSUE
113

OTHER BIKES FEATURED:
Gixer-engined GS lowrider, VN800 bob-job

WORDS: NIK
PIX: JOHN BRANDWOOD
MODEL: KERRY-LOUISE
(WWW.KERRY-LOUISE.CO.UK)

MONSTER MAX

THERE'S BEEN A LOT OF TALK IN CERTAIN CIRCLES RECENTLY ABOUT HOW THE BIG WHEEL BIKE THING IS OVER – HOW BOBBERS ARE NOW THE THING TO HAVE AND ANYTHING ELSE IS OLD HAT.

Tosh and pish, ladies and gentlemen, tosh and pish (he says in a poor impersonation of Stephen Fry). Bobbers are, indeed, things of automotive beauty, but they're not the be-all and end-all of custom bike building as some people would have you believe.

Take the motorcycle in front of you as an example. It couldn't be further removed from the bobber ethos and yet still be classed as a motorcycle, and I don't care how cool a bobber is - if you were to take any of them and park it on the street next to this thing, I don't think most people would even notice the bobber there. This thing is almost a caricature of a motorcycle – it's a bike that's been inflated and exaggerated in almost every way, shape and form and, as such, it has a 'presence' like practically no other motorcycle on the planet.

This bike is actually Johnboy's third and most over-the-top 'Max. The first one was completely and utterly stock, standard and just as the small lemon-coloured gentlemen at Yamaha intended. He sold that one on and bought another that had had a few bits done to it, but then he had the (mis?)fortune to meet Steve 'Mephistopheles' Taylor, the man

behind the country's leading purveyor of custom motorcycle parts for the 'Max, Taylormade Performance Engineering. And, like Faust, Johnboy was bewitched by the wonders he was offered and swiftly sold his soul to the smooth-talking Welsh devil. At first he opted for just a pair of Tribal 17" wheels and upside-down forks and, for a while, they sufficed. But once you're in the grasp of the demon, he'll never let you go and it wasn't long before Johnboy'd changed the 190 rear for a 280 and replaced the front with a 160 with bigger yokes to suit. They too did for a while but, still unsatisfied, he wanted more and swapped the wheels again, this

time for a 330 rear and a 200 front along with a monoshock conversion and, again, bigger yokes. He smoked about on it, won many trophies and had it featured in 100% Biker, but still he wasn't completely happy. That's the price when you sell your immortal soul, y'see – eternal torment.

He happened to mention to Steve one day that he'd seen a 'Max with a 360 rear in, but didn't like the way it hung out the back of the bike like a trailer. Steve consulted his grimoires and they ○

SPEC SHEET

ENGINE:

1986 Yamaha V-Max, polished & ported heads by PDQ, PDQ chain-drive conversion with billet outer cover, Dynojetted carbs, K&N filter in stock airbox, one-off right hand side 4-1 stainless exhaust by Dave Leonard, Tecno-Bike radiator cover

FRAME:

1986 Yamaha V-Max, modded swingarm pivots by PDQ, twin chain outrigger conversion, modified Taylormade Performance Engineering monoshock conversion, stock footrests & hangers

2009
Feb 19

ISSUE
113

OTHER BIKES FEATURED:
Gixer-engined GS lowrider, VN800 bob-job

> # In the end, though, they got it sorted and John would like to apologise to Glynn for (possibly) causing him a stress ulcer.

decided that, because of the sheer size of the 360 wheel and tyre, the only way to keep the bike short and in proportion was to convert it from shaft drive to chain. Mephis ... sorry ... Steve found a bike that had had just such a conversion and so Johnboy bought it and they broke it up and sold off all the bits that they weren't going to need (and 'Max number two too). They now had a basis to work from. Johnboy had a very definite idea of what he wanted, '240 front, radial brake upside-downies, a 360 rear that doesn't look like a hillclimber, all black with no polishing - I want it to stop traffic and to be able to ride like it's been stolen!' Right then.

The style of wheel he picked was a billet three-spoke Reaper thirteen inch wide eighteen incher with a Vee Rubber 'Monster' tyre. He also decided that he wanted a single-sided rear arm too. Thankfully he works for a company that has a ready supply of metal and he managed to persuade his boss, Steve, to supply him with enough raw material to allow Steve (Taylor) and his oppo Glynn to make him one using a Triumph hub and brake and an outrigger transfer shaft and secondary chain system too. This, of course, makes a feature of the right hand side of the wheel, exaggerating an already pretty damn fuggoff hoop to almost epic proportions.

Anyway, with the hard part done it should've been plain sailing from that point in ... or at least it would've been if Johnboy hadn't been struck with an almost terminal case

of the contraries – almost terminal in that he changed his mind so often that Glynn was ready to kill him. In the end, though, they got it sorted and John would like to apologise to Glynn for (possibly) causing him a stress ulcer. Taylormade's well-thumbed Tecno-Bike catalogue was pressed into service again, 'cos the Tecno-Bike stuff is luvverly, and from it they ordered a belly pan, a new radiator cover, fat and funky side panels and the monstrous Triple X dummy tank/air-scoops unit. The tail unit is a Taylormade MV-style one that's designed to accept the stock seats (both the front and rear) and the fuel filler bit that allows the stock underseat fuel tank to be filled up. Talking of this underseat area, you'll notice there's a distinct lack of rear shockerage on display – that's because, unlike most 'Maxes, Johnboy's 'Monster Max', as he has christened it, runs monoshock suspension rather than the more normal twin shockers. The conversion is one of Taylormade's and is a direct bolt-on fitment that, ●

SPEC SHEET

SHARP END:

Taylormade Performance Engineering 8x18" billet three spoke Reaper wheel, Metzeler 240/40/18 tyre, Braking Wave discs, 2006 Yamaha R1 radial calipers, extended 2006 Yamaha R1 upside-down forks with 63mm sleeves by Taylormade Performance Engineering, one-off Taylormade Performance Engineering billet yokes (three bolt top, six bolt bottom), tapered MX 'bars, stock switchgear, Beringer radial master-cylinders, HEL braided stainless steel brake lines, Moto Gadget digital instrument console

BLUNT END:

Taylormade Performance Engineering single-sided steel swingarm, Ohlins shock, Taylormade Performance Engineering 13x18" billet three spoke Reaper wheel, Triumph hub/caliper/disc, 360/30/18 Vee Rubber 'Monster' tyre

TINWARE:

Taylormade Performance Engineering front mudguard & Mantis headlight unit, Tecno-Bike Triple X dummy tank/scoops, stock tank, Taylormade Performance Engineering MV Augusta-style tailpiece with standard seats, Tecno-Bike side panels & bellypan

SPEC SHEET

ELECTRICS:
Modified stock loom, LED tail light with built-in rear indicators, Kellerman 'bar end front indicators

PAINT:
Satin black by Duncan's son

POLISHING:
Nope

POWDER COATING:
Swingarm by owner's mate, fork sleeves/ wheels by DC Services, Leominster (01568 610034)

ENGINEERING:
PDQ & Taylormade Performance Engineering

THANKS TO:
'Steve & Glynn at Taylormade Performance Engineering (01597 860692 or www. taylormade-wheels. co.uk); Larry & lads at PDQ Motorcycle Developments (01753 730043 or www.pdq1. co.uk); Dave Leonard (07780 6263061); Benny at Tecno-Bike (www. tecno-bike.com); the gorgeous Cathy for the hassle/tea/food,; the equally, if not more, gorgeous Michelle (my wife); & Duncan's son for the paint ...'

cleverly, allows the use of the stock Yamaha fuel tank. The shock itself is an Ohlins multi-adjustable mega-expensive unit – nothing but the best on this bike.

The next item on the list to be dealt with was the 240 front wheel. Yep, that's right, a 240 front wheel. Now I don't know about you, but I don't even have a wheel that wide on the back of any of my bikes (the TL has a 190 and the Harris has a 180), let alone on the front and, for many folk who see these big wheel bikes, it's actually the wideness of the front hoop that has the more profound effect on them. Big back wheels, you see, have almost become the norm these days, but big front ones still knock people back on their heels because there aren't that many of them about. Johnboy's front is a madder-than-a-mad-thing eight inch wide eighteen inch Reaper billet three spoker and it has genuine Braking Wave discs (none o' yer cheapy aftermarket copies 'ere) and state-

> **A radially-mounted caliper (as opposed to a conventionally-mounted one) is stiffer, you see, and is better at maintaining alignment with the disc.**

of-the-art radial calipers. Whaty what whats? Radial calipers, guv – like wot they put on all modern sports bikes. A radially-mounted caliper (as opposed to a conventionally-mounted one) is stiffer, you see, and is better at maintaining alignment with the disc. This means the pads stay in alignment better, making better contact with the disc and so exerting less side-to-side force on it while generating less heat too. With traditional caliper mounts on the trailing end of the caliper, pad pressure at the leading edge of the caliper has considerable leverage to twist the caliper - radial mounting takes care of that. Putting a mount at both the leading and trailing end

of the caliper means leverage at the leading edge of the pads is reduced to a level that it becomes insignificant. Got that? Good, there may be questions later. Anyway, these particular radial brakes came from a 2006 Yamaha R1 and they mount directly onto a set of upside-down forks from the same model. These have been extended (usd's are always shorter than rwu's, remember?) and slotted into gert fat billet yokes with almost as many pinch bolts as there are in the wheels – three each side on the top 'un and six each side onn the bottom. Yes, we all know that two pinch bolts on each one could probably have done a perfectly adequate job, but they wouldn't have looked anywhere near as fuggoff, would they? The only problem with having yokes of such immensity is that they

make the forks themselves look a bit weedy, but that was easily solved – Taylormade made up some 63mm sleeves to go over the top of them. Sorted, what's next?

Dave Leonard in Bristol made up the stunning right hand side pipework for the exhaust system (as he does on all Taylormade projects), and the front mudguard is one of Taylormade's very German-style items. The headlight unit (or fairing or whatever you want to call it) is also one of theirs, and the 'bars are tapered motocross ones with deeply desirable Beringer master-cylinders mounted on them. Not seen the Beringers?

They're like ISR ones, but sexier ... if you can conceive of a master-cylinder actually being sexy. Shall we move on?

The bike was nearly done as the annual V-Max bash at Baskerville Hall in Hay-on-Wye approached and, as Johnboy wanted to unveil it there, his good mate Duncan's son worked all night to paint it. It is, as any fule can see, painted in the correct colour for all motorcycles – matt black ... okay, so maybe it's more satin than matt, but the thought was there. Sadly, Johnboy's talking about spraying it Ford Focus orange when he gets a minute spare. Hmm, another orange

V-Max, that's original ...

Steve, Glynn and Faust ... sorry, sorry Johnboy had to van the finished bike to Baskerville as they hadn't been able to get a 'plate made up in time but, fear not, this thing is no trailer-queen – they got it out of the van to shocked appreciation from the assembled 'Max masses, fired it up and gave it a big fistful and found, to their delight, it wheelspins in the first four gears in the wet. Cool. They also found that it peppered Shaggy's car with chippings quite nicely too ... oops, sorry Shag. ✖

2008
Feb 21

ISSUE
100

OTHER BIKES FEATURED:
1926 Rudge, Hongdou 200, Exile Harleys

UNMISTAKE A-BUELL

WORDS: NIK PIX: JOHN BRANDV
MODEL: BECKY JO HAYHURST

ALTHOUGH IT MAY NOT LOOK OR SOUND LIKE IT THE WAY WE DESCRIBE IT HERE IN 100% BIKER, BUILDING CUSTOM BIKES IS HARD WORK.

Designing and building your own custom motorcycle or trike from scratch is a big commitment to undertake and not everyone who starts a project, no matter how good their intentions, is able to finish it. For every bike that appears in this magazine in all its completed coolness,

there are at least another five sitting in sheds and garages around the land unfinished due their owners' lack of money, time and, quite often, interest.

Let me use myself as an example. I currently have eight motorcycles registered as belonging to me and, amazingly, of those eight I now actually have four that both work and have MoTs.

It's taken me the best part of nearly three years to get them sorted due to either not having the time or the money or, sadly, the fact that I possess the equivalent mechanical skills as a creature born without opposable thumbs. I've had or got the designs for 'em worked out in me head for ages, but the lack of dosh, time or an ability to use a spanner

It turned out that what he had in front of him was an S1 White Lightning Buell, the slightly hopped-up version of the stock hooligan torque beast S1.

|||||||||||||||||||||||||||||||||||||||||||||||||||

without sticking it in me own eye means that everything proceeds at a pace that makes the passage of galactic time seem positively speedy. The only difference between me and those who given up on their projects as either a bad job or totally unrealistic is that I'm not that smart – I will get all mine finished ... one day.

Of course there is something good to be made from all these people who've given up on their bikes and that is the fact that, if they've even the slightest bit of nous about them, then they've usually done the major work needed to get a project going before they give up. Now I know that might sound a little odd to anyone out there who hasn't built a bike, but it's a sad fact that of life that it's the last ten or fifteen percent of a build that will break a project's back – it's the fiddly little jobs that are the soul-destroying ones. Once you've done the big jobs - like the frame mods and the wheel/suspension or engine transplants, made your yokes and sorted out your tank - it feels like there's only a few days work more to be done because the bike sort o' looks finished. It's only when you've been sitting in your shed for three weeks

trying to get your minimal wiring loom to do exactly what it's s'posed to do or you've re-made the headlight brackets for the umpteenth time and you suddenly realise that you've still not stripped the bike for powder coating or got everything ready for paint and Summer's almost here and all your mates are coming round to show you their new bikes while yours is still weeks of hard work away from being done ... well, that's when the resolve weakens and, inevitably, the 'unfinished project – just needs paint, electrics and a few minor jobs' adverts start to appear in the

free ads of your local paper.

As long as you're aware that there's still a fair amount of work to be done when you read such an advert, then buying an unfinished project can be a good way of getting yourself a cracking custom bike on the road without quite as much effort as starting from scratch. Simon 'Unky' Butler, the owner of the super-tough Buell in front of you, knows this because that's exactly what he did with this 'ere bike. He'd had a Buell a few years back and really regretted selling it so when he was told of one that'd had a fair amount of work done to it ◗

SPEC SHEET

ENGINE

Buell S1 White Lightning, gas-flowed Thunderstorm heads, big valves, titanium collars, Mad Dog Racing rollers, Screamin' Eagle valve springs, Wiseco 1310cc big bore kit, one-off twin choke carb with one-off trumpets, strengthened crank, Barnet heavy-duty clutch, Baker six speed gearbox, Compufire ignition, one-off straight-through exhaust by Zorstec, Wizards of NOS' 40bhp single-stage nitrous oxide-injection kit, Nasty Bikes belt pulley, one-off outrigger plate by owner & Dockside Superbikes

FRAME

Buell S1 White Lightning, widened to fit swingarm by Dockside Superbikes, one-off polished sub frame by Dockside Superbikes, modified Vortex Yamaha R6 rearsets

SHARP END

Sixteen inch Revtech Aerofoil wheel, one-off Braking Wave discs, Harrison Billet Honda RC30-spec six pot calipers, one-off caliper hangers, re-worked & gold-nitrided black anodised WP usd forks, one-off wider billet yokes by Dockside Superbikes, one-off 'bars by GCS, Zodiac race controls, one-off master-cylinder reservoirs by owner, one-off switchgear by owner, Moto Gadget digital rev-counter & speedo

2008
Feb 21

ISSUE
100

OTHER BIKES FEATURED:
1926 Rudge, Hongdou 200, Exile Harleys

that was languishing unloved in someone's workshop, he jumped at the chance to lay his greasy paws on it. He popped along to see it and was more than a little impressed with what he saw so a deal was done and the Buell and all its goodies went home with him.

It turned out, after further inspection, that what he had in front of him was an S1 White Lightning Buell, the slightly hopped-up version of the stock hooligan torque beast S1. The frame'd been widened to fit a one-off twin rail swingarm and a fat 250 section wheel and tyre, and the stock forks'd been replaced with all-singing, all-dancing WP items. It now also had a beautiful alloy sub frame and the beginnings of a very clever oil tank cum tail piece, and a whole host of other goodies too. In fact, as I said often happens, most of the big jobs'd been done – all he really had to do was break out a big tube of Evostick and glue it all together. Okay, so that's oversimplifying it a bit (I'm a master of understatement, me), but that was the principle anyway. So, he rolled up his sleeves, spat on his hands and in a true Fred Dibnah stylee, set about building up what is probably the trickest example of Uncle Erik's street scorchers to ever turn a wheel here in Blighty.

The idea behind the original modifications was to get a huge rear wheel stuck up the S1's jacksie. Previous matey

had taken the frame down to Polygon/PEST Engineering down in deepest dampest Gloucestershire to have them work their magic over it. Polygon/PEST have built themselves a strong reputation as being a crew who really know what they're talking about in the streetfighting word and the few alloy framed-bikes they did have as much cred as their Harris or Spondon counterparts. There have been a few changes there recently and they've changed their name to Dockside Superbikes, but they're still doing frame and suspension etc modifications to the same unbelievably high standards as before. They opened the frame up and made an outrigger plate to transfer the drive from the motor to the new larger Revtech rear wheel, and also handcrafted one of their luvverly twin-rail alloy swingarms to attach it to the frame too. And while they were at it, they made up the sub frame with its adjustable

rose joints so that it can be raised or lowered depending on the look Unky wants that day. The linkage to the Penske shock is rose-jointed as well so it too can be raised or lowered and this, of course, means that the bike's geometry can be changed – lengthened or shortened – depending on whether Unky wants to leather it round the bends or tear-arse down the drag strip.

Up front, as I said, the usd forks have been changed to WP ones and the three spoke front wheel replaced with another Revtech one to match the rear. The only slight problem with this was that because the wheels are actually designed for Harley-Davidsons rather than Buells and come in a sixteen inch front and eighteen inch rear fitment, rather than the seventeen/seventeen ensemble that is generally reckoned to be the optimum for handling these days, nothing in the aftermarket range for Buells'd actually fit. He ended up having to get one-off discs made by Braking and ultra-rare RC30 Honda-spec race calipers from Harrison/Radial, one-off caliper hangers to attach them to the WP forks and, of course, a high profile front tyre to bring the wheel's diameter back up to that of a seventeen incher and so not handle like a shopping trolley. Dockside had made up the yokes, and Gaz at the now sadly defunct GCS made ○

> **He'd had a Buell a few years back and really regretted selling it so when he was told of one that'd had a fair amount of work done to it he jumped at the chance to lay his greasy paws on it.**

BLUNT END

One-off alloy twin-rail swingarm by Dockside Superbikes, Penske shock, eighteen inch Revtech Aerofoil wheel with 250 section tyre, one-off Braking Wave disc, ISR mini caliper, one-off torque arm by owner, aftermarket belt, Revtech Aerofoil pulley

TINWARE

Buell carbon fibre front mudguard, stock fuel tank, one-off seat by owner, one-off tail-piece incorporating oil tank

ELECTRICS

Modified stock loom by owner, 'alien' headlight, LED rear light

PAINT

Black with blue pearlescent ghost flames by Dean Hibbard at AFM (07968 698167)

POLISHING

Kerne

ENGINEERING

Stainless fasteners throughout, one-off hidden brackets etc

THANKS TO

'My bank manager; Gaz at the now sadly defunct GCS; the guys at Dockside Superbikes (http://www.applegate.co.uk/indexes/telcode/all-01452.htm 01452 380883 or www.docksidesuperbikes.co.uk); Kerne, the god of all chrome & polishing; Dean; Dai; Junk; & all my mates for not abandoning me while I was stuck in the garage...'

up the very wide and very German-style 'bars that sit atop them.

Sitting just behind all that is a built-to-the-hilt and nitrous'd Buell motor. Originally made for a Canadian race team, only the bottom end had been assembled when Unky got his hands on it. It'd got a strengthened crank, a six speed Baker 'box and a heavy-duty clutch inserted into its cases and to them our Unky added gas-flowed Thunderstorm heads with big valves and titanium collars, Mad Dog Racing rollers and Screamin' Eagle valve springs and a Wiseco 1310cc big bore kit. Fuel is delivered to the cylinders by a truly one-off carburettor with no needles and no jets that was designed by a very clever guy who, in effect,

made it work like a fuel-injection system. The bottom part of the carb controls the slow-speed running and then as the revs rise, the upper part starts to inject fuel in too. It's a very simple and effective design and it works well but, as Unky says, it is really a race carb and so is a little bit lumpy at low revs.

The turbo looky-likey exhaust system on the other side of the motor is the work of Biker's old mate Andy at Zorstec and is, like all his work, beautifully made and unfeasibly bastard loud.

I'm really not kidding – Unky fired it up outside the studio and in the confinement of the

I'm really not kidding, Unky fired it up outside the studio and in the confinement of the little car park the noise was positively orgasmic.

little car park the noise was positively orgasmic. Whether the Old Bill in his native Burton-on-Trent think the same thing, though, is another matter ...

The motor's crowning glory is a single-stage nitrous oxide-injection system. At the flick of a switch, the Wizards of NOS kit dumps a full forty horsepower into the system and the Buell leaps forward like a starship going into hyperspace. Unky must have a very good grip, that's all I can say, 'cos with 'bars that wide and 40 bee-aich-pee of gas being dumped into the already kick-arse engine he's going to need it!

Thankfully, when the bike does take off like a Friesian with a firework up its fanny (please don't ask me how I know this ...), the kick-up on the home-made seat and seat unit helps him to stay aboard. The seat unit itself is worthy of note – styled on a Ducati Monster rear seat cover (which, he said smugly, is something that, as

far as I know, I was the first person to use as a tail piece on my Moto Martin back in about 1997), it also contains an integral oil tank. Buell motors, like H-Ds, are dry sumpers and so need an external oil tank, but the frame mods to get the big back wheel in meant that there wasn't room to mount one in a conventional position so, cleverly, it's been incorporated into the seat unit.

That really just leaves the rear hoop, doesn't it? Oh, and the paint too, but we'll come to that in a moment. The wheel is, as I said, an eighteen inch item

that wears a 250 rear tyre and the braking is a combination of another one-off Braking Wave disc and a so-sexy-it-hurts ISR mini caliper by the Swedish stopper maestros. Unky made the torque arm to control it, and also modified the aftermarket rearsets, that were originally intended for a Yamaha R6, but look way better here, that operate it. The rear pulley is a Revtech Aerofoil to match the wheel and the front 'un is a Nasty Bikes one that's attached to the owner-modified Dockside outrigger arrangement.

Dean Hibbard laid on the deep and glossy black paint with its subtle pearl blue ghost flames, and Kerne polished and chromed all the bits that've been polished and chromed, and that, pretty much, was that. Unky's had the bike on the road since the Spring of last year, alongside his gorgeous XJR1400 turbo (you can really go off people, can't you?), and has picked up so many awards for it that he's had to put an Akro under his mantelpiece to stop it dropping down onto the hearth and killing his cat. Don't get him wrong, though, this thing i'n't no trailer queen – he rides it. If you were at last year's Farmyard mudfest, you'll have seen it up there covered in more kak than even the most dedicated bog snorkeller and, he says, it took him three days to get it all off when he got home.

Lovely bike, Unky, thanks for letting us photograph it! ✪

The idea behind the original modifications was to get a huge rear wheel stuck up the S1's jacksie.

WORDS: **SPINDLE**
PIX: **JOHN BRANDWOOD**
MODEL: **GEMMA HILES**

FIFTY-SEVEN

I FIRST MET BENNY FROM BONESHAKER CHOPPERS A FEW YEARS BACK WHEN I TURNED UP AT HIS SHOP ON A CHOPPER HE HAD BUILT A LONG WAY BACK AND WAS MET BY A TALL SKINNY BLOKE WITH FOUR FOOT LONG DREADLOCKS, COVERED IN TATTOOS, AND MORE FACIAL PIERCING THAN A MUPPET PLAYING WITH A BUCKSHOT CARTRIDGE.

I was kinda scared as he ran towards me with his dreads flowing in the Summer breeze. Then he spoke, 'Yow royt, Spindle?' Well, that's all I could understand - he sounded like Noddy Holder on speed.

It turns out the bloke that commissioned the originally XS650 build had used it as a showpiece in his garage and occasionally fired it up for the benefit of his mates, but never actually ridden it. I had managed to track the owner down and made him an offer on the bike, got it home, gave it a service and then rode the

hell out of it for a few years.

I hooked up with Benny and Co at a few meets following that first meeting and we all got on well - we had the same taste in bikes and the same taste in getting steaming drunk. On one of the memorable occasions me, Benny,

Neil, Bobby Mercury, Scotty Cowboy, Sumo and Jonny Cool all went to the National Drag Meet at Long Marston Raceway and we fired up the bikes in the middle of the night for a little ride around the site,

> "I wanted mid-controls on my bike because my short little legs won't reach forwards. So I took a little trip to Halford's and bought a pair of BMX stunt pegs and the Boneshaker lads modified them to fit."

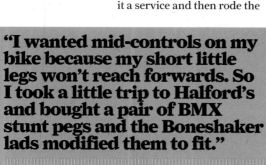

much to the dismay of the miserable bastard hotrodders camping next to us who threatened to set us on fire with petrol. Okay, in hindsight it was a little out of order, but it was funny as fuck at the time.

I became a regular hangout at the shop and kept all amused with my funny Northern accent and dialect. I sound like Jack Duckworth, according to

Bobby Mercury and Scotty Cowboy who often raised my concerns with their 'manlove' - on regular occasions they mounted each other and simulated anal sex ... must be a Midlands thing. We got to talking about building me a new bike - Benny was about to do a project/feature in American V magazine and it was to be time-lapsed on video and publicly shown on U-Tube. The project was named 'The Great British Bobber Budget Build-Off' and Benny and another well-known shop were the challengers. I liked the sound of this and fought bravely with Benny to secure a price I could afford when the bike was built. Once the deal was done, we threw some ideas about the workshop - I thought that silver flake and a rear whitewall would be cool but Benny, being Benny, just smiled and completely ignored all my ideas and proceeded to build the coolest bike from his shop to date. ◗

SPEC SHEET

ENGINE
Harley-Davidson 883 Sportster, bellmouth air-filter, twin spark ignition, modified 2" drag 'pipes by Boneshaker Choppers

FRAME
Flyrite Choppers Smokin' Gun rigid frame, 33 degree rake, 2" stretch, stock H-D foot controls with Halfords BMX stunt pegs

SHARP END
Flyrite Choppers ribbed 21" tyre/chrome 40 spoke wheel/disc/caliper/4" under DNA springers/ three inch risers, braided stainless steel brake line, H-D master-cylinder (polished), Boneshaker Choppers twisted Z-bars, chrome mini speedo, one-off stainless switchgear panel by Boneshaker Choppers, Supersixties yellow flake grips

BLUNT END
Flyrite Choppers 16" chrome 40 spoke wheel/ sprocket brake/Shinko tyre/NeveRust stainless steel rear mudguard strut

2008
Aug 7

ISSUE
106

OTHER BIKES FEATURED:
Phat-wheeled V-Max, 250 Beezer, 750/4 chop

SPEC SHEET

TINWARE

Flyrite Choppers Sportster-style tank with one-off brass filler cap, one-off hand-tooled leather seat by Deb Lawson with Flyrite Choppers springs, modified Flyrite Choppers rear mudguard, modified Twisted Choppers oil tank, one-off battery box by Boneshaker Choppers

ELECTRICS

One-off loom by Ian from Second City, 4" Bates headlight on Flyrite Choppers bracket, billet Iron Cross rear light/side-mount numberplate

PAINT

Gold flake over black by Punch at G&C Cycleworks

POWDER COATING

Frame via Boneshaker Choppers

POLISHING

Boneshaker Choppers

THANKS TO

'All at Boneshaker Choppers (www.boneshakerchoppers.co.uk or 01527 575934) – Benny (Noddy Holder impressions & spanners), Scotty Cowboy (spanners), Bobby Mercury (spanners), Neil the short-haired hippy (spanners) & Vicky, tea girl & chip shop chick; Deb for the seat; Ian for the electrics; & Punch for the paint ...'

As Boneshakers are the sole distributor for the Flyrite Choppers range of budget bikes, they decided to use one of their kits to get started. They ordered in a Smokin' Gun rolling chassis – a rigid frame, a 21" front wheel and brake, a 16" rear wheel with sprocket brake, a set of springer forks, a Sporty-style tank, a back mudguard with stainless rear struts and a few more bits too – because the FRC rollers are a good, solid, well-designed basis for building a bike with plenty of scope to make it your own. They're also super low (which is good because I'm only little) and, equally importantly, they are cheeeeeap. Benny and Co normally build their own frames, but the FRC roller was perfect for this project.

They then scored a cheap 883 Sportster motor from their friend Ian, stripped it of any dull bits and polished them in-house. Me being a truck driver for a living, I brought the brass fuel cap, which is a diesel cap off a belly tank off a refrigeration trailer similar to what I drive. It was the only contribution Benny would allow me – that might sound harsh, I know, but this was something he was building as part of a competition so it had to be right and, as he has been doing this a lot longer than me, I was happy to bow to his judgement. The finished bike is as cool as hell and it won the comp (more on that in a mo') so he must've done something right, mustn't he? Anyway, Benny had to make a new filler neck to take the cap and TIG it in to place.

The oil tank was an eBay

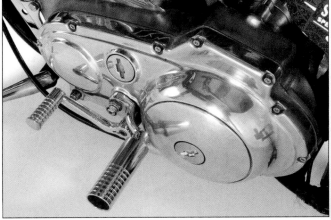

score - originally a Twisted Choppers item, Benny had to cut it to fit around the centre post of the frame – and Boneshaker Choppers made up the little tucked away battery box too.

Benny also engineered a new top mount for the engine to house a couple of stainless switches and ignition barrel, and also several brackets and bosses were manufactured to hold stuff together.

I wanted mid-controls on my bike because my short little legs won't reach forwards. So I took a little trip to Halford's and bought a pair of BMX stunt pegs and the Boneshaker lads modified them to fit. The 'bars are off-the-shelf twisted zeds and the 'grips are yellow flake Super Sixties.

Punch at G&C handled the paint and turned out a top job again using gold flake over a black base, and laying down the 57 on the tank and the 'SO/CAL' logo on the oil tank by hand. The seat was covered and hand carved by Deb Lawson who does all Benny's seats (she's the best

> **"It ran as smooth as silk and it returns reasonable fuel consumption and, most importantly, it's as cool as a polar bear's arse to ride."**

I have seen in this country), and Scotty Cowboy and Bobby Mercury helped with the final build. Ian at Second City handled the wiring and the bike fired up sweetly and just took a little jetting to get right. It now runs as smooth as silk and it returns reasonable fuel consumption and, most importantly, it's as cool as a polar bear's arse to ride. ✪

2009
Dec 24

ISSUE
124

OTHER BIKES FEATURED:
Kawasaki chopper

THE CONFEDERATE

FRANK BEESLEY IS THE EX-LANDLORD OF THE BIKER PUB NIK USED TO DRINK IN YEARS AGO. HE ALSO BUILDS A PRETTY MEAN BIKE TOO.

I n over fifty years of riding motorcycles, there are not many makes that I haven't owned or ridden, but a notable exception is my all time favourite - the Indian, the real American motorcycle.

With examples of Indian 4s selling for £40,000 plus, though, it looked as if I had no realistic chance of owning one either but, as I have something of a record of building rather nice custom bikes, I decided to

build my own and, although there would be a nod to the Indian, it wasn't going to be a slavish copy - rather, it would be a bike that would've been a competitor to an Indian 4 if it had been made in 1929.

My bikes tend to grow organically, so I set out the basic parameters and let it grow from there. Time was totally irrelevant, but money wasn't as I had just retired and had

plenty of one but none of the other. With this in mind, it was decided that anything that could be made 'in house' would be, using materials that were readily available.

It was intended that it would be a practical useable bike and not a 'shiny-shiny' show bike and, in keeping with the 1929 theme, it would have very little chrome. The one departure from this concept from the start was that it would have disc brakes in order to be useable with modern traffic. It would also be shaft drive, as I could make a transfer box, but not a bevel box. The smallest, lightest

and most authentic-looking engine available was going to be a Reliant and I obtained one in exchange for building a trike out of a CX500 for a friend.

All of these decisions and design parameters took place over about a year before I even picked up a spanner or cut a piece of metal. The first thing to build was a jig to build the frame and from there things could proceed as and when I had spare cash, usually obtained by working on other people's bikes.

The engine was overhauled and set in the jig and the frame built around it. The forks are my design, based on the Indian layout but using modern technology such as needle roller bearings, and the leaf spring was modified from a discarded Land Rover unit.

I wanted to keep the handlebars as uncluttered as possible so, to operate the front disc, I used a BMW ❍

2009
Dec 24

ISSUE
124

OTHER BIKES FEATURED:
Kawasaki chopper

"I painted it (and most of my shed, me and anything else in a fifty yard radius) myself."

SPEC SHEET

ENGINE:

Reliant Regal, SU carb from Morris Minor, one-off air-filter by owner, Formula 750 clutch & ignition, converted three speed gearbox, one-off stainless exhaust system by owner, Goodridge oil lines to remote oil filter

FRAME:

One-off by owner, one-off footboards & controls by owner

SHARP END:

Unknown Russian wheel & brake, one-off forks by owner with needle roller bearings & Land Rover spring, one-off yokes by owner, one-off Goodridge braided stainless steel brake lines, one-off handlebars by owner, BMW cable-operated master-cylinder hidden under tank to keep 'bars clear, replica vintage switchgear & clocks

remote master-cylinder from a breaker mounted under the tank. I also didn't want an oil filter sticking out from the engine so I built a dummy oil tank and hid a remote filter inside it, along with the electrics. The battery box was made by a local retired carpenter (the 'old gits network' has its uses), and the induction and exhaust were totally redesigned with very pleasing results.

By now it was starting to take shape, and turning out better than I had hoped. All nuts and bolts are stainless as I am too lazy to keep cleaning things (throughout,

the nuts and bolts are in keeping with the period and no Phillips or Allen head screws were used), and other items 'recycled' include a seat base made from a tractor seat and a headlamp mount made from a supermarket shopping trolley. The rubber mats on ◗

2009
Dec 24

ISSUE
124

OTHER BIKES FEATURED:
Kawasaki chopper

SPEC SHEET

BLUNT END:

Ural Cossack wheel/brake/modified front master-cylinder, one-off shaft drive via transfer box to offset shaft by owner

TINWARE:

Modified trailer mudguard as front mudguard, one-off petrol tank by owner, replica Massey-Ferguson seat base modified to suit & upholstered locally, modified trailer rear mudguard, one-off dummy oil tank by owner, one-off polished mahogany battery box by local retired carpenter

ELECTRICS:

One-off loom by owner, vintage replica headlight, replica Vincent Black Shadow tail-light

PAINT:

Brilliant Red by owner

ENGINEERING:

All work except battery box by owner

THANKS TO:

'Paul Beesley, my son & the world's best welder ...'

> "The rubber mats on the footboards came from the darts mat at my local pub and the clutch pedal was made from a piece of metal that I found in a lay-by."

the footboards came from the darts mat at my local pub, the clutch pedal was made from a piece of metal that I found in a lay-by, and the rear wheel and drive came from a Cossack, a custom version of the Russian Ural. I never found out where the front wheel had come from.

The rear master-cylinder was modified from a front master cylinder from an unspecified Eastern European bike as it was small enough to hide, while the mudguards were intended for a utility trailer, and the sheet metal to make the tank was left over from a US Marines ambulance that I had restored for a museum.

As it was not intended that it would be a show bike, I painted it (and, it has to be said, most of my shed, me and anything else in a fifty yard radius) myself and the finish is entirely authentic looking. It had to have a name so, based on my interest in the American Civil War, I called it 'The Confederate'. I later found out that there is a bike company called that registered in the USA, so my apologies to them if they are in anyway offended by my effort.

I like to think that it shows what can be achieved without just throwing money at a project, and I look forward to spending the rest of my retirement building bikes for me and anyone else who wants one. ✪

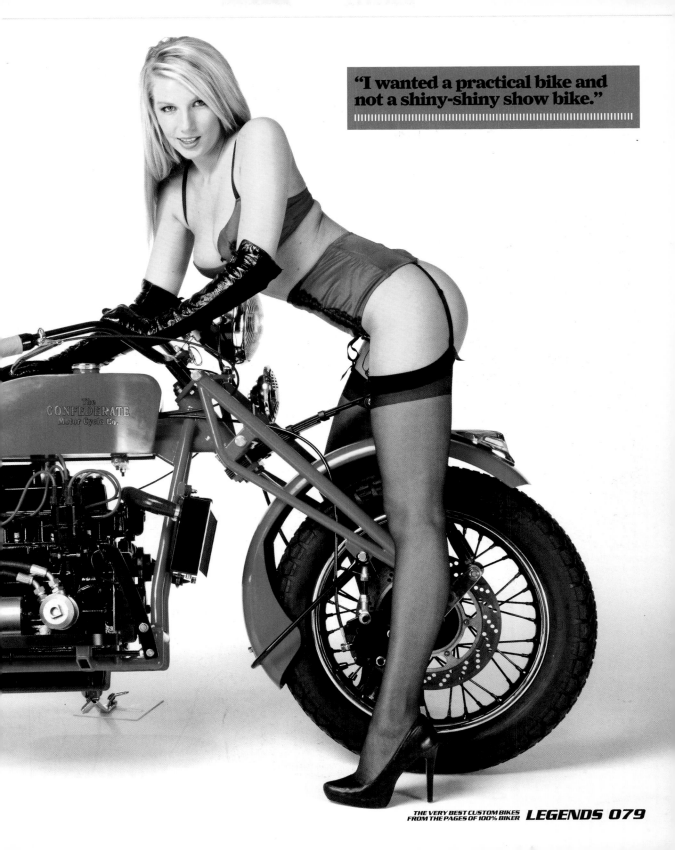

"I wanted a practical bike and not a shiny-shiny show bike."

2008
Oct 2

ISSUE
108

OTHER BIKES FEATURED:
Streetfighter GSX-R, Framed 1000RX

PERFECTLY

WORDS: PC
PIX: JOHN BRANDWOOD
MODEL: RACHEL C

THIS BIKE BUILD WAS INSPIRED BY SEEING THE BARON'S SPEED SHOP BOBBER 'THE DELINQUENT'. I DECIDED THERE AND THEN THAT I WOULD BUILD MYSELF A BOBBER. THERE WAS ONLY ONE SLIGHT PROBLEM – TO DATE, THE EXTENT OF MY MECHANICAL EXPERIENCE WAS HAVING THE TOP END OFF A HONDA 125 ABOUT TWENTY FIVE YEARS AGO.

CREATED

I had a 1978 XS650 that was my daily ride to work at the time, so off the road it came and out came the spanners. I gave myself two years to finish the build, aiming for the 16th June 2008. The first job was to pull the bike apart and decide what I was keeping and what I was replacing. It didn't take that long

and soon I was looking at what remained of my XS all over the garage floor. That was it – I was in it up to my neck now.

The engine, obviously, was staying so I stripped it, replaced anything that needed doing (got the replacement parts from 'gasehound' on eBay – they've got everything!), fitted an electronic ignition to make starting a little easier and had the carbs aqua bead blasted by Motalia. I then put mesh-mouthed bell-mouths on to finish them off.

I wanted it to be a hardtail because bobbers are always hardtails, aren't they? I had thought of having a complete frame made and rang Dave The Frame in Birmingham to find out how much one would cost. We chatted for a while and he convinced me that I didn't need a complete frame and that he could do me a very nice

weld-on hardtail and so, for the very reasonable price of two and a half hundred quid, the hardtail was fitted to the stock frame and a great job he made of it too. While I was there I got him to make me up a set of straight-through exhausts too that, again, he made a great job of.

I used eBay as major source for components and got some really good deals on stuff. The front wheel came from there – it's a twenty one inch Sun alloy rim from a KTM twin-shock dirt bike and came with a tiny six inch single-sided KTM drum brake. It had to be a drum brake because, I think, bobbers just don't look right with disc front brakes. I had it laced up with stainless spokes and fitted with a very old skool Avon Speedmaster MKII ribbed tyre, and it's been slotted into the stock XS fork legs. There was still something about it that didn't look quite right, though, it didn't look old enough ... if you see what I mean? I solved this by buying a set of Triumph (or BSA, can't remember which) rear springs off eBay, cutting them down to the right size ○

SPEC SHEET

ENGINE

1978 Yamaha XS 650SE, stripped, cleaned, painted & rebuilt, electronic ignition fitted, carbs aqua-cleaned by Motalia (0870 7 664152), rebuilt & re-jetted, meshed bell-mouths, re-chromed straight-through slash-cut exhausts by Dave The Frame

FRAME

1978 Yamaha XS 650SE, hardtailed by Dave The Frame (0121 360 0400)

SHARP END

Twenty one inch Sun polished alloy rim, stainless spokes, Avon Speedmaster MK II ribbed tyre, KTM six inch single-sided brake drum, magnesium brake plate, standard fork stanchions chromed & re-ground by AM Philpot (01582 571234), Triumph/BSA rear shock springs cut to size & fitted between polished & chromed yokes, chromed standard risers, Vincent 'straight' 'bars, Triumph/BSA grips & levers, one-off stainless headlight bracket

BLUNT END

Standard sixteen inch polished alloy wheel rim, stainless spokes, Avon Speedmaster MK II tyre, standard brake drum, one-off drilled stainless torque arm, one-off stainless rear brake switch holder, one-off chromed side-mount numberplate holder

TINWARE

H-D Sportster petrol tank with Triumph/BSA taps repositioned to rear, leather seat from eBay USA with five inch springs, unidentified rear mudguard from Stafford Show, one-off stainless rear mudguard stays, stainless electrics box with H-D ignition & Shellmex brass petrol cap

2008
Oct 2

ISSUE
108

OTHER BIKES FEATURED:
Streetfighter GSX-R, Framed 1000RX

SPEC SHEET

ELECTRICS

One-off loom by Steve at 'Indy's Daydream' (01257 231808), Bates-type headlight with peak, Vincent rear light

PAINT

Nissan metallic orange & Toyota metallic black by Simon at Spraytech (0161 723 5981)

POWDER COATING

F&M Powdercoatings (01772 700414)

POLISHING & PLATING

Leigh Polishers (01204-861022)

ENGINEERING

All work done by owner, anything hard by Simon & Andy

THANKS TO

'My other half, Pat, for not moaning about the time & cost of finishing the bike; the dogs for keeping me company in the garage & nicking my tools; the boys at Yateson's Stainless for their help & advice (01204 370099); & family and friends (especially the Greerys) for giving me support & encouragement when I couldn't see any light at the end of a bloody long tunnel! This bike is dedicated to my dad, Brian, who by the way is still with us ...'

> **"It's surprisingly comfortable to ride, although you have to permanently remember that the front brake is not much more effective in stopping the bike than trying to stop by putting your bare feet flat on the tarmac."**

and sliding them over the tops of the fork legs between the two chromed yokes. A peaked Bates headlight (on a one-off stainless mount that I'm very proud of) and a pair of Vincent straight 'bars with Triumph (again, or BSA) grips and levers finished off the front end and I was ready to move on.

I got a Sportster tank for a good price and fitted it with old British fuel taps that I moved to the back of the tank so that I'd get a bit more range out of it. The seat's an old-style leather one I got off American eBay and fitted with the bits of the cut-down springs I hadn't used on the fork legs. Any welds that were stress-bearing were done by others who made it look easy - anything simple I learned how to do myself ... thank God for angle grinders and another run or two of weld! The

electrics box is made from stainless and fitted with an ignition from a Harley and a brass Shellmex petrol cap – I wanted it to look like an oil tank, even though the XS doesn't actually need one, because bobbers should have oil tanks, shouldn't they?

The back mudguard came from the Stafford Show (I don't know what it's off) and I modified it to fit closely round the rear tyre 'cos that's what looks right. The stays are stainless one-offs, and the wheel itself is the standard XS one polished and re-laced with stainless spokes. I made the torque arms, the holder for the rear brake switch and the

side-mount number plate holder with its Vincent rear light too.

Simon at Spraytech lacquered and polished the slightly Exile-style Nissan metallic orange and Toyota metallic black paint, and F&M Powdercoatings did the frame black. Leigh Polishers did the polishing and plating, of which there is a lot, and Yateson's Stainless provided all the fasteners.

The electrics were the last job to be sorted and I had been estimated several hundred pounds to do the job. I happened to start a thread on a Border Terrier forum about the build and a person I had met a couple of times posted that if I needed any help with the electrics he would help me out. Seeing as how electricity is a complete mystery to me I told him that if he thought he could do the job and his price was right, the job was his. A couple of hundred quid and the cost of the components later I had a completely re-wired bobber that started about six kicks later. This guy helps to wire airplanes for a living, so it was no surprise when he made short work of my XS.

That was it - despite several breaks of up to a couple of months the bike was

started up two days under two years later. I had a bit of trouble getting the bike to run properly after the build was completed, but changing the pilot jetting has sorted that out, and it now just needs some fine tuning to the carbs to make it 100%. It's surprisingly comfortable to ride, although you have to permanently remember that the front brake is not much more effective in stopping the bike than trying to stop by putting your bare feet flat on the tarmac - it does look cool, though, and that was what I wanted in the build.

As an aside, if anyone is thinking of starting a build but, like myself, they don't really have the expertise - just get on with it and carry it through! It's a great feeling when it's completed and if I can do it, anyone who can hold a spanner can. ✪

2008
Oct 30

ISSUE
109

OTHER BIKES FEATURED:
B72 Stateside ironhead sporty, GSX750

WHITE MAGIC

I'D LIKE TO START THIS ARTICLE, IF I MAY, BY OFFERING YOU A LITTLE ADVICE GLEANED OVER MANY YEARS – IF YOU'RE THINKING ABOUT HAVING HUMAN FACES PAINTED ON ANY PART OF YOUR MOTORCYCLE OR MOTORTRICYCLE, BE VERY, VERY CAREFUL WHO YOU PICK TO DO IT FOR YOU.

2008
Oct 30

ISSUE
109

OTHER BIKES FEATURED:
B72 Stateside ironhead sporty, GSX750

Carpathian from Ghostbusters II, while others have, a little uncharitably perhaps, asked if it's a self-portrait of Panda? Anyway, whatever it is, Spread likes it and that's all that counts, isn't it?

His 'Max has been an on-going project for a couple of years now and, despite (or perhaps because of) taking all that time, has come out an absolute stunner. It's based on a 1998 'Max which has been extensively modified. The front loop of the frame is pretty much as was, but the rear section has been chopped about quite dramatically – the swingarm area has been re-worked and the stock 'arm, which incorporates the drive-shaft, removed and replaced with a purpose-built one by Mike at Madswingarms that's been lengthened seven inches to suit and widened to take

You see, while there are many very good custom painters out there, doing true-to-life pictures of people is a skill that only a few of them have. Ty Lawler at Pageant Paint is very good at people, as is Piers Dowell and Andy at Hairy Designs and whoever it was who painted that 'Buffy The Vampire Slayer' cruiser that was going around a year or so ago, but some others, no matter how good they may be at everything else, struggle a little to get the proportions of a face just so.

What has this got to do with the rather fcuk-off V-Max you see here in front of you? Well, Simon Green, or Spread as he's

more commonly known, also has a face painted on the front mudguard of his bike too but, to be quite honest, he doesn't actually know why it's there in the first place – he'd originally just asked Panda at Liquid FX for some black flames over a white base, but you know these artistic types ... Panda sent a pic across to Spread of the face he'd just done on his front 'guard asking him whether he liked it or not, and Spread said 'yup' so that was it. Spread to this day doesn't really know what the inspiration behind it was – some folk have said it looks a little bit like Vigo The

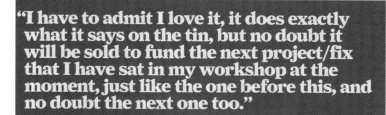

the massive 300-section rear tyre. Hagon shocks replace the stock 'Max ones and their mounting points have been moved from the conventional place to a new inboard setting where they almost act like a monoshock. This, as well as actually working, helps tidy up the rear end a treat and, with nothing to obstruct your view of it, emphasises the sheer size of the rear wheel. The wheel itself is an Image Wheels eighteen incher that's been built onto a one-off hub by Blings, polished until it shines like the arse of a policeman's trousers and then clear ceramic-coated so that Spread doesn't ever have to polish it until it shines like the arse of a policeman's trousers again. The rear brake is an underslung Yamaha R1 item on a one-off under-slung caliper bracket from Custom V-Max Services, the torque arm is a one-off from Blings, and the rear brake master-cylinder has been given a

quick makeover courtesy of a Rizoma billet reservoir.

An equally lavish amount of attention has been spent on the bike's front end too. The stock right-way-up forks n' stuff have all been removed in favour of a complete FZR 1000 EXUP RU ensemble – seventeen inch front wheel, 320mm discs, six piston calipers, re-valved upside-down forks. Blings machined up a set of chunky billet yokes with a Moto-Gadget digital display unit set inside the top one. The 'bars are also one-offs by Blings, and the switchgear is Max stuff painted white, while the clutch and brake master-cylinders are Nissin remote ones with Rizoma reservoirs. Lastly, the front tyre is an oversize 130 Avon to give the whole front a little bulk.

The same Eff-Zed-Arr that supplied the forks n' wheel n' stuff also gave up its front mudguard, and that startling and eerie-looking sculpted tank cover is from the legendary Tecno-Bike in ›

SPEC SHEET

ENGINE:

1998 Yamaha V-Max 1200, Dynojet Stage 1, K&N air-filter, one-off 4-2 exhausts by Zorstec

FRAME:

1998 Yamaha V-Max 1200, re-worked subframe, suspension mounts moved, ABM rearsets

SHARP END:

Avon 130/70/17 tyre, Yamaha FZR 1000RU EXUP wheel/discs/six pot calipers/usd forks, one-off slab yokes with integral Moto-Gadget digital speedometer by Blings, HEL white braided steel brake lines, one-off handlebars by Blings, Nissin remote master-cylinders with Rizoma reservoirs, standard switchgear painted white

BLUNT END:

One-off extended swinging arm by Madswingarms, re-sprung Hagon Nitro shocks, ceramic coated Image Wheels eighteen inch with Metzeler 300 tyre, aftermarket disc, Yamaha R1 rear caliper underslung on caliper hanger from Custom V-Max Services (www.customvmaxservices.co.uk), stock master-cylinder with Rizoma reservoir, one-off torque arm by Blings

2008
Oct 30

ISSUE
109

OTHER BIKES FEATURED:
B72 Stateside ironhead sporty, GSX750

SPEC SHEET

TINWARE:

Yamaha FZR 1000RU EXUP front mudguard, Tecno-Bike (www.tecno-bike.com) faux tank cover, lowered stock seat, stock underseat fuel tank, one-off Ducati 916-style seat unit, Vmaxparts side panels (www.vmaxparts.co.uk), V-Maxbits' bellypan (www.vmaxbits.com)

ELECTRICS:

Modified stock loom with alarm/remote start & sat nav, three Tecno-Bike headlights, Tecno-Bike Shark tail-light, front indicators from V-Maxbits, rear indicators from box in shed

PAINT:

White & black by Panda from Liquid FX (www.sprayliquidfx.com or 07765 444472)

POLISHING/PLATING:

Rear hubs by Simon the plater, clip-ons by Blings, & ceramic coating on rear wheel by Image Wheels (www.imagewheels.co.uk)

ENGINEERING:

Yokes/clip-ons/swingarm/handlebars/torque arm/drive hubs/disc carrier by Blings & Madswingarms (all available via vmaxparts)

THANKS TO:

'Steve for sourcing a lot of bits for me from Europe; the Mad Turnip for being on the end of the 'phone with all his technical help; Mike at Madswingarms for all his help; Marshall for the help with picking me up in van after blowing up engine & spending the best part of weekend helping replace said engine; & all my mates for their help ...'

Belgium. The single seat is the stock 'Max one, albeit lowered, and the stock 'Max underseat tank is still there too, while the tail-piece is a Ducati 916-style one that's been made specially for this bike and the side-panels and bellypan came from vmaxparts.co.uk and vmaxbits.com respectively. Technique Finishing took care of powdercoating all the white bits ... err, white and, as I've already said, Panda at Liquid FX did the airbrush magic thang adding all the flames, scales and other subtle little touches that you may at first not notice.

Spread had intended to get the bike on the road by the Spring of 2007 but, like all builds, it had its fair share of hold-ups and he finally got it MoT'd and taxed just in time for the Southern Comfort V-Max Rally in July '07. He rode it there and he rode it home ... and that's pretty much where it stayed for the rest of the year 'cos it scared the shit out of him. It had, you see, originally been built with a 360 rear and Spread quickly found that he'd made a major mistake with the front end set-up mixed with the rear end set-up - it would not do corners ... no, he really means it would NOT do corners! He had two options - scrap the front end and start again or scrap the back end and start again so.

So he removed the 360 set-up and sold it and, after a few months (okay, so it was July 2008), what you see is what came out of the workshop.

He took it out on its maiden voyage and was very impressed with the new rear end's handling – it tracked straight and true and didn't try and spit him off if he attempted a turn. Sorted – he'd cracked it.

2000 plus miles later, it's been all over the country and the Continent and picked up five trophies and it's still running very well and, most importantly, taking corners better than

he'd ever dreamt a 'Max with a big back end would. He says, 'I have to admit I love it, it does exactly what it says on the tin, but no doubt it will be sold to fund the next project/fix that I have sat in my workshop at the moment, just like the one before this, and no doubt the next one too will be sold on for when I need another fix too ... and so on and so on... but that's what we do, isn't it? Shed builders unite!' Couldn't have put it better myself, mate! ⊗

2008
Nov 27

ISSUE
110

OTHER BIKES FEATURED:
German Intruder, XS Café racer, Norfolk Triumph

OLD ENGLISH CUSTOM

WORDS: MR MOO
PIX: CLINTON@STUDIOTHREE.ORG
MODEL: SAMANTHA BUXTON
(WWW.SAMANTHABUXTON.COM)

I already had a couple of SP370 motors hanging around so that was my starting point. I also had a set of damaged custom springers, basically just fit for parts. That's it - the project began.

I stripped and saved what I wanted off the springers (the springs and front legs) and remade the rear legs styling them on a Harley 45 pattern. Made my own top and bottom yokes, rockers, handlebars (with a Honda internal throttle) and anything else needed. The fork crown is made up from nineteen individual bits to get the cast appearance I required, and the front wheel is a CB750/4 rear wheel hub with

WELL, TO START WITH THE BIKE IS GREAT – IT'S LOW AND IT LOOKS SO OLD AND IT'S STAYING WITH ME AND MY 650 YAM/BSA BECAUSE THEY'RE PROPER-LOOKING TRADITIONAL HYBRIDS.

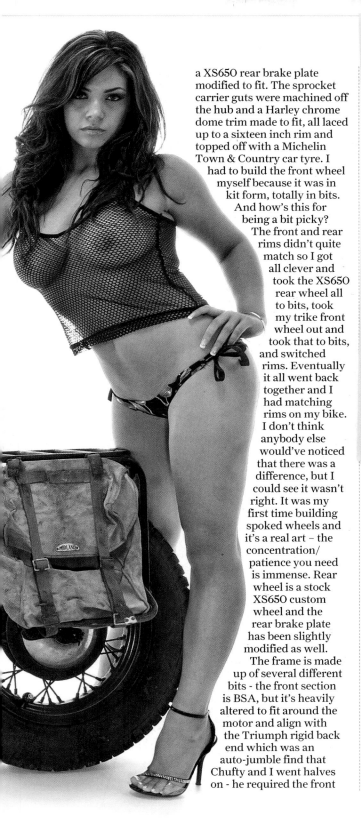

a XS650 rear brake plate modified to fit. The sprocket carrier guts were machined off the hub and a Harley chrome dome trim made to fit, all laced up to a sixteen inch rim and topped off with a Michelin Town & Country car tyre. I had to build the front wheel myself because it was in kit form, totally in bits. And how's this for being a bit picky? The front and rear rims didn't quite match so I got all clever and took the XS650 rear wheel all to bits, took my trike front wheel out and took that to bits, and switched rims. Eventually it all went back together and I had matching rims on my bike. I don't think anybody else would've noticed that there was a difference, but I could see it wasn't right. It was my first time building spoked wheels and it's a real art – the concentration/patience you need is immense. Rear wheel is a stock XS650 custom wheel and the rear brake plate has been slightly modified as well.

The frame is made up of several different bits - the front section is BSA, but it's heavily altered to fit around the motor and align with the Triumph rigid back end which was an auto-jumble find that Chufty and I went halves on - he required the front frame rails and castings and I wanted the rigid backend, so he sawed it in half. The candy twist front down tube is also a combined experiment by Chufty and myself - we didn't get it right first time, in fact we did it about seven times before it was right. I know I could've gone out and bought a bit of pre-twisted metal and saved myself a load of time, but where's the fun in that? I fabricated my own engine plates and added some sidecar lugs to the frame as well as making up my own castings on the frame too.

The petrol tank and the oil tank are from jumbles, and the toolbox from my mate Ted. They're all genuine BSA items. The rear mudguard was the best ever find, sat on a mate's scrap pile in his back garden ○

SPEC SHEET

ENGINE:

1979 Suzuki SP370, Amal 932 MK1 Concentric carb with bellmouth on homemade inlet manifold, homemade exhaust (two Suzuki T500 downpipes & Harley fishtail), Suzuki GSX 400 front sprocket, homemade hand gear-change, homemade kickstart

FRAME:

1946 BSA B31 front half with 1950s Triumph 5T rigid back end, homemade candy-twist front downtube, front frame section heavily modified to fit around engine & to mate up with Triumph rigid back end, modified old British footrests & hangers, homemade engine plates

SHARP END:

Michelin 500-16 Town & Country car tyre, Honda 750/4 rear hub with modified Yamaha XS650 brake-plate & modified Harley chrome dome trim, sixteen inch rim, homemade springers with homemade yokes, homemade handlebars from a set of scrap bars fitted with Honda internal throttle, Reliant handbrake outers as clutch & brake cables, British brake & clutch levers on homemade mounts welded to handlebars & matching choke lever from a lawnmower

BLUNT END:

Yamaha XS650 Custom wheel, Avon SM 500-16 tyre with painted-on white wall (that turned creamy for some reason after I painted it), homemade rear brake lever made form different sizes of chain links welded into shape, old spanner as torque arm

"The front racks were added when the bike was on the road, as I had to be able to carry my stuff about. I like to be able to use the stuff I build - if I can't strap crap all over it, it ain't no good to me."

(thanks Ben). The headlight is an old car spotlight lens and rim attached to a modified Bates shell with a rib welded on the back to match the rear 'guard. The taillight is Austin A30 with a LED conversion and red lens off a lathe, I think, or some form of machinery. The seat base came from Ted and I cut and reshaped it, mounting it on old pushbike seat springs. I then got Alan at Saxon Seats to cover the base in foam and leather, leaving it unfinished for me to stitch up and make the rear seat trim as I wanted to have a go myself.

All the paintwork and lining on the bike I did myself - matt black with just a touch of BSA maroon to break it up and give it an old appearance, finishing it off with grey lining. Another mate, Skin from Airy Art Airbrush Studio, did the 'Genuine Junk Parts' logo on the mudguard and what a smart job he did for me, it's fucking perfect. The logo came about because I like hotrod stuff as well and the logo is a proper Ed 'Big Daddy' Roth one from the 1960s. I thought it was appropriate because I had used so much second-hand, damaged, scrap parts or just pure junk to some people but, as I could see a use for them, the logo was a perfect finishing touch.

I also had a go at pistriping, but it isn't that easy and doesn't just happen overnight – there's so much to learn about it: Techniques; quality of paint; how you use the paint;

brushes and looking after brushes; let alone learning how to hold the brushes properly. Pin striping is a real art that takes years to learn to be able to pick up a brush and do it straight away. I only managed a few simple lines on the headlight shell and top yoke, although I did have a go on the petrol tank, but it just looked a load of shit. I did, though, manage to write the name, Bessie, on the left hand bottom corner of the petrol tank.

I made my own British-style battery carrier using a dummy Exide battery case, squeezing a modern battery inside it. Most of the electrics are hidden inside the oil tank running the alternator wire through the

dummy oil line and the rear light wires through the frame tube. There're a couple of small switches at the bottom of the headlight shell, the other main switches are on the backside of the oil tank and the kids helped me plait the headlight wires.

I didn't like the standard Suzuki left hand engine cover so I used a damaged BSA primary cover and altered it to fit (thanks Ted for the primary cover). I also altered the petrol tank, moving the petrol cap from the centre to the top right and adding the speedo housing in on the left hand side to balance it up and finishing it off with a centre rib to match the rear guard headlight shell. I made my own inlet manifold and used an Amal ○

Pin striping is a real art that takes years to learn to be able to pick up a brush and do it straight away. I only managed a few simple lines on the headlight shell and top yoke, although I did have a go on the petrol tank, but it just looked a load of shit.

2008
Nov 27

ISSUE
110

OTHER BIKES FEATURED:
German Intruder, XS Café racer, Norfolk Triumph

I made my own British-style battery carrier using a dummy Exide battery case, squeezing a modern battery inside it.

||||||||||||||||||||||||||||||||||||||||||||||||||||||||||||||||||||||||||

932 Concentric carb because I couldn't get the original SP370 carb to fit; it was all a bit snug. I did my own curly copper fuel lines - it took more than several attempts to get this right, and I was getting pissed off with myself and the amount of copper pipe I wasted too.

I made my own old traditional-looking speedo drive utilising a Kawasaki KR1S ninety degree drive off the back of the clock, adding a brass end and grease nipple and making my own mount so that it was adjustable, and it's driven off the rear drive chain. The exhaust is made up from two Suzuki T500 down pipes and a Harley fishtail. The down pipes had to be cut and welded to get the correct angle I wanted, but basically they were the right diameter to match the fishtail.

The rear brake lever is made up

There are actually five cut up conrods and three spanners on the bike here and there, don't ask me why but I just did

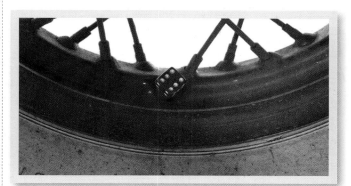

of various different oddments of chain – I also had to make a couple bits of link myself so that it tapers down in size, and it was then welded into the shape I required. I used an old scrap spanner as a rear brake torque arm. The hand change was quite involved - there are over twenty individual bits including a Reliant gear change, an old Kawasaki torque arm, a bit of a

Honda centre stand and some different types of brake plate arms, and a piece from a lathe. All of it was junk, but they all have that old cast appearance about them. Then came the job of making it all go together and look right - that was another task in itself. I also needed to make a kick start as well - I used a Suzuki rear brake lever because the splines were the same as the SP370 kick start shaft and welded the rear brake lever splined section to an old British kick start lever, also making up my own kick start pedal out of chain.

I machined my own bullet shell/cartridges to fit the ends of my rear fork legs to finish it off to give a little bit more character. The brake and clutch levers are British, but fitted to home-made lever mounts welded onto the 'bars with a matching choke lever from a lawn mower. The brake and clutch cables are made from old Reliant handbrake outers, yet another scrap bin find.

I added a little bit of brass and copper here and there to the bike to give that old look. There are actually five cut up

conrods and three spanners on the bike here and there, don't ask me why but I just did. The front racks were added when the bike was on the road, as I had to be able to carry my stuff about. I like to be able to use the stuff I build - if I can't strap crap all over it, it ain't no good to me. ✪

SPEC SHEET

TINWARE:
BSA B31 fuel tank modified to take Smiths chronometric speedo/ retunneled to sit right on frame/seam welded down middle/filler cap moved, homemade speedo drive, LE Velocette seat base modified & reshaped to fit, twisted pushbike seat springs, old British rear mudguard, homemade British-style battery carrier, BSA oil tank as electrics box, BSA toolbox

ELECTRICS:
Homemade loom by owner, most hidden inside oil tank, wiring through frame for tail light, alternator wires in oil line, homemade headlight from old car spotlight glass & rim/ modified Bates shell with rib welded on back to match petrol tank & rear 'guard, modified Austin A30 side light with LEDs fitted inside & red lens from lathe handmade to fit, horn & high/low switch in headlight shell, ignition & main light switch in back of oil tank, plaited wires to headlight, dummy Exide battery case with modern battery inside

PAINT:
Matt black & BSA maroon/grey lining on wheels & tinware/proper BSA transfers on petrol tank & oil tank by owner, 'Genuine Junk Parts' logo artwork by Skin at Airy Arts Airbrush Studio (www.airyarts. co.uk or 07708 391014)

ENGINEERING:
All by owner

2009
Aug 6

ISSUE
119

OTHER BIKES FEATURED:
USA customs supplement, GSX-R streetfighter

FAT ATTACK

PHIL PIPER OF CHOPPERSHACK IS ONE OF THE COUNTRY'S LEADING BIKE BUILDERS AND HE, LIKE US, HAS A BIT OF A THING ABOUT EXILE CYCLES-STYLED BIKES. PIX BY THE LATE CLINTON SMITH RIP

This bike came about as a result of a previous bike I built for an old school mate of mine, John T, back in 2006 – a sort of replica of the Exile Cycles 'Dragster'. He has a best mate called Paul who lives in the same town in the North East and they are both heavily into bikes, cars and anything else fitted with an internal combustion engine.

Whilst perusing the Exile Cycles website the pair came

across one of Russell's bikes that he'd called the 'Fat Bloke' and John convinced Paul that his life wouldn't be complete without a replica of the self-same bike. 'Right! We'd better ring Phil' says John, 'he's good mates with Russell and he'll be able to get us all the bits at a good price'. Duly summoned, I 'phoned Russell and ordered all the parts needed. Several weeks later all the things landed at the Choppershack World Headquarters and the pair drove down from the far north and loaded up their trusty Tranny van with all the parts. 'Err, you do know it's not a kit, don't you?' I told them, 'it's lots of hard work, nothing will fit and you'll need to be able to weld, use a lathe and fabricate lots of parts'. That's the thing about

'I don't think he appreciated just how rapid a two litre engine hooked up to a six speed tranny would be. As he says, when you wind it up everything else goes backwards'

Exile bikes – they might be seen as 'kit' bikes, but they're not – they're really really not, you have to build them yourself just like you would any other chopper. 'No problem', they said – famous last words! Two weeks later I got the expected 'phone call, 'Err, Phil, do you think you could put it together for us?' After saying 'told you so' several times, I told them to bring all the parts back to me to stitch together. In fairness they're both busy men and

didn't realise quite how much work would be involved.

Anyway, in between times Paul had changed his mind about some features of the bike and now didn't want an exact replica of the 'Fat Bloke'. That's not a problem for me, I'm used to that here, but the bike turned out to be far from straight forward. The frame is an Exile Softail and the forwards are Exile parts too, but they were just about the ●

SPEC SHEET

ENGINE:

120 cu in (2 litre) Ultima, Choppershack air cleaner & points cover, modified Exile Cycles Monster pipes, 3" BDL belt primary drive, six speed Ultima gearbox

FRAME:

Exile Cycles Softail, Exile Cycles forward controls

SHARP END:

Exile Cycles 200x15" wheel/twin discs, SJP four pot calipers & Fat Glide forks & yokes, Choppershack risers, Early Glide handlebars with internal throttle, Jaybrake controls

BLUNT END:

Exile Cycles 230x15" wheel & sprocket brake assembly, Choppershack dummy hub & rear light/number plate assembly

TINWARE:

Modified Exile Cycles front mudguard, 6 gallon fatbobs with one-off stainless centre strip by Choppershack, Le Pera seat, modified Exile Cycles oil tank, modified Exile Cycles rear mudguard with Choppershack struts

2009
Aug 6

ISSUE
119

OTHER BIKES FEATURED:
USA customs supplement, GSX-R streetfighter

ELECTRICS:

One-off loom by
Choppershack,
dechromed billet
headlight with
built-in dipswitch

PAINT:

Black with silver
ghost flames by John
Coopers Artworks

**DECHROMING
DULL CHROMING
SATIN
POLISHING:**

Honest Kern's
Polishing Services

ENGINEERING:

All welding/fabrication/
hydraulics/oil lines/one-off
parts/brackets/spacers
etc by Choppershack

THANKS TO:

'John T; Russell & Paul
at Exile Cycles; & Phil at
Choppershack (www.
choppershack.com)

only parts (except perhaps for the sprocket brake too) that didn't need to be 'adjusted' to get the bike right. The 120 cubic inch (that's two litres in English money) Ultima engine is fitted with a six speed gearbox and a three inch BDL primary, and dressed with one of my trademark Choppershack air cleaners and a Choppershack points cover too while the 'pipes are big bore Exile Monsters.

Up front there's an Exile fifteen inch wheel with a 200 tyre, twin Exile discs and a pair of SJP four pot calipers. The forks are also SJP, but Fat Glides with SJP yokes and vintage-looking Early Glide handlebars with an internal throttle, of course. I used Jaybrake controls because they're good, and a billet headlight with a built-in dipswitch (it didn't stay looking 'billet' for long though, as you'll see in a minute).

Six gallon fatbobs fill the space above the engine properly (the tank strip was made by me), while the seat is a trusty Le Pera. Both mudguards are Exile ones that I modified to sit right (the rear one's struts are by me), and I also played around with the Exile oil tank too. Another fifteen inch wheel, this time with a 230 tyre, sits below the rear 'guard and uses an Exile sprocket brake, while the numberplate/rear light is a Choppershack one.

Dry build completed, it was off to the usual suspects for finishes. John Cooper's the man around these parts for top quality paint jobs and he didn't disappoint here – a deep black that you can almost fall into with subtle silver ghost flames.

All of the alloy

components were stripped down and taken to Honest Kern's Polishing Emporium not for polishing, but to be made dull. The job infuriated 'Da Kern' who ranted, 'people pay me to make things

'You gonna buy that bloody bike or just stand there looking at it all day?'

shiny, not bloody dull!', but he still did a top quality job. The handlebars and 'pipes etc were treated to a special satin chrome finish normally reserved for certain vintage bikes - it's a finish not many can do, but Kern rose to the challenge and did another top job.

All back to yours truly and it was down to me to assemble it, wire it, do the hydraulics, the oil lines etc etc – all the bits that really take the time. It was soon all done, though, and the big day approached. I went to fire it up – press the button, everything goes round ... but the motor won't start! I went back through it all again and, eventually, traced the problem to a faulty ignition processor. I got on the blower to the supplier and a replacement arrived two days later - get it fitted, reset the timing, hit the button and, bingo, first prod it fires into life! The maiden voyage was successful and the bike was comfortable and definitely fast. Off down the MoT station and it sails through the test (as it should do, it's practically a new bike!).

Several days later I delivered the bike to Paul and John way oop north and they're blown away with the finished machine - 'more than happy' is the expression. Paul took the bike out for a test spin and, twenty minutes later, John and I are a bit worried when he hasn't come back. Half an hour later, though, he hoves into view with a big grin on his face. Yep, he loves it. He's now ridden the bike many times and loves it to death. ⊗

2009
Sept 3

ISSUE
120

OTHER BIKES FEATURED:
Swedish lowrider, Two Triumphs, Shovel head chop

FOR YOFFI...

THIS BIKE ORIGINALLY BELONGED TO DARREN 'YOFFI' MULLINDER BEFORE HE WAS TRAGICALLY KILLED. DEREK DE REUCK TELLS US ABOUT HIS BIKE. PIX BY THE LATE CLINTON SMITH RIP

I wanted to dedicate this feature to my friend Darren Mulliner. For those who didn't know Darren, he was a hugely popular salesman at Dockgate 20 Harley Davidson in Southampton, and was tragically taken from us last year when he collided with a lorry riding to a bike event near Wisbech.

The story began when, after years of knowing Darren while working in a rival bike shop myself, we crossed paths time and again to trade stock and refer customers. Darren was always happy to help, no matter what it was for. Paula, my wife, had finally agreed to join me on the road and not sit behind me any more and, when the time came after 22 years

as my pillion, there was nobody better to sort out the right bike for her than him.

So off we went to Dockgate 20 to see what the boys had and, after an hour or so, Darren, and his colleague Red Thetford, came up with the perfect bike for her. There aren't too many bike shops around that can inspire a female rider to buy a new bike and not patronise her like a kid, but Darren had that talent - as we stood there deliberating like yer

'I resolved to ride it with respect and reverence to a great friend I will always remember and not change it too far from the vision he had'

do, he walked straight up to Paula, put his arm round her and said in his cheeky way, 'You gonna buy that bloody bike or just stand there looking at it all day?' Sold!

After a week of excitement and calls to Darren to get the registration done in time, the following Sunday was the day to go over and collect her new pride and joy. The morning dawned, we went

over to Southampton ready to ride away her new Sportster and as we walked up to the door Red, the sales manager, came out, met us outside and broke the coldest news I have ever had to take - Darren had collected a lorry coming the other way on a ride-out the very day before and they couldn't revive him. Wwe stood still in shock for what seemed like an age - nothing ◐

SPEC SHEET

ORIGINAL YEAR, MAKE & MODEL:

2002 Harley-Davidson FLSTF Fat Boy

ENGINE:

Harley-Davidson 1450 Twin Cam, Mikuni HSR42 carb, Arlen Ness Big Sucker air-filter, one-off hand-built exhausts by Attitude Customs with copper heat-shields & wrap by owner

FRAME:

2002 Harley-Davidson FLSTF Fat Boy, new rear section by Attitude Customs, stock forwards

SHARP END:

130/70/16 Metzeler tyre, 16x4" stainless rim, billet hub, 5mm stainless spokes, chrome CCI discs, stock calipers, stock forks with Arlen Ness lowering kit, stock yokes, Goodridge brake lines, Sportster 883 Hugger 'bars (eBay), stock master-cylinders/switchgear

BLUNT END:

Stock swingarm, stock shocks with Arlen Ness lowering kit, 16x7" stainless rim, offset billet hub, 5mm stainless spokes, 180/50/16 Metzeler tyre, CCI disc, stock caliper, pulley machined to clear rim & tyre, stock belt

TINWARE:

Cut-down stock mudguard, stock tank/dash/clock, steel-based tractor seat with springs locked up with internal bolts, one-off handmade rear mudguard by Attitude Customs, one-off handmade electrics panel under seat by Attitude Customs, one-off handmade side-mount 'plate & light holder by owner

2009
Sept 3

ISSUE
120

OTHER BIKES FEATURED:
Swedish lowrider, Two Triumphs, Shovel head chop

ELECTRICS:
Stock main loom & headlight, LED cat's-eye tail light, LED bullet-style indicators

PAINT:
One-off Willow Green mix close to Sunbeam/Bantam green initially by Andy Peters at Jeez Louise, then Dave at Customise Perfection (01794 322686)

POWDER COATING:
Rims/hubs, battery cover by Trestan Finishers

ENGINEERING:
Custom fabricated battery & electrics cover/rear 'guard/front 'guard/exhausts/side-mount 'plate by Attitude Customs & owner

THANKS TO:
'Tony Tate & Red Thetford at Dockgate 20 for the initial deal; the whole team at DG20 for their support & encouragement notably Darren's sister Julie for her kind permission to commemorate my old mate Darren in this feature; Simon Harris at Attitude Customs (07758 241123 or www.attitude-customs.co.uk); & most of all my beautiful wife Paula for putting up with 24 years of my incessant bike habit, never objecting to the money & time I have invested in a lifetime so far of riding, building, crashing & fixing bikes & for having the courage & determination to join me on the road on her own Harley last year, a Sportster Darren himself sold her one week before he was taken from us ...'

I tried to say would come out without choking me and Paula was in bits. We eventually regained some composure and got the paperwork done, and took the bike home still numb that the world had been robbed of such a huge lovable character, a man I didn't even realise I thought so much of - his kindness and spirit went deep and ran through you like water, touching every part of your consciousness. I miss you, mate, and God knows I always will.

As time went on, we would often make our regular visit to the shop for coffee and a browse and, one particular Sunday two months later, we went in and on a podium for sale was Darren's bike. I couldn't believe my eyes. The reason it suddenly appeared now was that, while he was riding it about, he had decided on a raft of custom improvements and sent it, with a list of demands, down to the house of fabulous fabrication 'Attitude Customs' in Woolston. While it was there Si Harris had taken the gas axe to the rear seat rails and fabricated the excellent

'You gonna buy that bloody bike or just stand there looking at it all day?'

rear tyre-hugging 'guard and carried out a host of other mods that'd taken it closer to what it is now. Darren had sent the bike in for the work and was tragically killed while it was there - he never saw it finished.

Now custom shops are very special places and custom builders are very special people - if we had to pay at main dealer rates for what they do, then a custom built chopper would cost over a hundred grand. They do it because they love it and none proved more so than on this

occasion - all the work Darren had asked for had been almost done when the news of his death reached Si who, to give him all the credit in the world, could have stopped work

there and then knowing he wasn't going to get paid for his labours. Instead, though, he calmly finished the bike and handed it back to Dockgate with no bill - bugger all, a simple gift to the family!

Within half an hour of seeing the bike there I had signed the invoice and the Fat Boy was mine. It was a mix of madness and panic - I just had to have it. I still can't explain why - I just wanted it, like yer do. I set out to make a few more improvements and stamp my own signature, as is usual when you buy a custom already done, but more than all I resolved to ride it with respect and reverence to a great friend I will always remember, and not change it too far from the vision he had.

I didn't really set out to change much other than the odd detail but, gradually, I did little things that added up to the bike you see before you. The 'pipes were wrapped in white heat tape which always gets dirty and looks crap, so I re-wrapped 'em in black. They still needed some more heat protection, though, so I chose pure copper 'cos it

looks cool. I discovered very quickly, though, that copper is more a heat sink than a heat shield ... DOH! It actually made it ten times worse, but by then it looked so trick I didn't want to change them so I just backed them with some heat padding underneath

and put up with a sweaty right leg.

I decided to lower it too. When I got the bike it was the regular Fat Boy ride height so I slammed it using an Arlen Ness lowering kit, taking two inches out of the front and three inches out of the rear. This immediately cost me all my ground ◗

2009
Sept 3

ISSUE
120

OTHER BIKES FEATURED:
Swedish lowrider, Two Triumphs, Shovel head chop

104 LEGENDS THE VERY BEST CUSTOM BIKES
FROM THE PAGES OF 100% BIKER

clearance but, after a bit of practice (like all things), I got used to it. The main gain is that it's so stable now you can lock the throttle off at eighty and fold your arms - love it!

The 'plate mount was more of an exercise in fabrication - it wasn't even meant to go on the bike, but it came together right, and I wanted something of my own style to add to the mix. The copper plumbing tube to carry the wiring is there because I love to have something that costs just 50p on every bike I have – it just keeps the old feet on the ground, you know? And the holes on the top of the light hood are in homage to the 'lake bed' hot-rodders who cut holes in their screen hoods to let the light in. When it was finally finished I took it down to Si Harris to show him what I'd done - my version of the finished bike. He spent a long time looking at it and then stamped me card in approval. Thanks mate, from you that's praise indeed!

No matter what we achieve in this life, how well we do in business or our careers, no matter how big your house, your car or your mortgage, life and people, I've found, are really all that matters. If I gave up my bike today and never rode one again, I know I'll always be a better man for having known Darren Mulliner and, whatever else I do in my life, I will try to make the choices in the happy-go-lucky and fun way he did - life's too short to get stressed about things. 'Take each day that comes as a gift' was the

No matter what we achieve in this life, how well we do in business or our careers, no matter how big your house, your car or your mortgage, life and people, I've found, are really all that matters.

way he looked at it and he was right. Wherever you are, mate, I'll never forget you.

And now, writing this a year on from the whole business and buying of both bikes, Paula and I rode 300 miles in a day on the anniversary of his death, partly to take her mum out for a birthday lunch, but mainly to celebrate what your bike is for - riding and enjoying. And somewhere along the five hours of motorways and A-roads we both made sure we reminded ourselves how soon it can end and how important friends and family are. Cheers.

One final thing – Darren's nickname that he used on Internet forums was 'YOFFI', an acronym for 'Young Offensive Fat Fuckin Idiot', and it was brilliant to hear it being explained at the inquest - the witnesses were saying 'I was riding behind Yoffi etc etc ...' when the judge or coroner or whatever he was asked, 'so who is this Yoffi person?' 'It's an acronym-style nickname, M'Lud.' 'Standing for what?' The court took a few minutes to settle down after that ... ⊗

2009
Nov 26

ISSUE
123

OTHER BIKES FEATURED:
Sportster bobber, V-Max, Bandit streetfighter

HARDASS HARDTAIL

ANDY COOPER HAS HAD A FEW OF HIS BIKES IN BIKER BEFORE, AND THEY'RE USUALLY ALL FJ1200-BASED. CAN YOU GUESS WHAT MOTOR'S IN THIS ONE? PIX BY JOHN BRANDWOOD, LONG-LEGGED LOVELINESS BY IRYNA.

SPEC SHEET

ORIGINAL YEAR, MAKE & MODEL:

1986 Yamaha FJ1200

ENGINE:

Yamaha FJ1200 1TX, K&N conical filters, aftermarket ignition switch, one off stainless steel exhaust by owner

FRAME:

One-off hardtail frame using engine as stressed member by owner, one-off stainless footrests & controls by owner

SHARP END:

Yamaha FJ1200 wheel, Yamaha FZR1000 discs, Suzuki GSX-R 750 calipers, Suzuki GSX-R 750 usd forks & bottom yoke, one-off billet alloy top yoke by owner, braided stainless steel brake lines, one-off stainless handlebars by owner, Aprilia Mille master- cylinders, micro toggle & push button switches, aftermarket mini speedo

BLUNT END:

Honda three spoke wheel & disc, Suzuki caliper, Yamaha FJ1200 master-cylinder, one-off stainless torque arm by owner

Andy Cooper bought a non running FJ1200 for the paltry sum of £50 with a plan to build a chop to sell on and make a few quid. After about four months, and with most of the fabrication done, he realised he'd totally lost interest in it so, one night just before Christmas, he went into the shed and, in his own words, 'cut the fucker up!'

He knew he wanted something radical so he set about creating something just that – radical! He'd picked up the GSX-R upside-down forks at the Newark autojumble a while back but, although they'd come with a bottom yoke, there's was no top one. Fortunately the firm he works for has a water jet profiler so he was able to draw a new yoke up and get it cut out there and, utilising the stock FJ wheel, a pair of FZR1000 discs and some Gixer calipers donated by a mate, that was the front end sorted.

Next thing he needed was a back wheel and a local breaker, Mark at Manic Motorcycles, sorted him out a Honda one that matched the front for a very good price. With these item stashed securely in his workshop, he was then able to start on a frame. He says he was quite worried because he'd not built a frame this radical before but, as it happens, it turned out to be one of the easiest parts of the build and he's really pleased with the way it's turned out. As you can see looking at it, although it looks at first glance as though it's a monoshock'd trellis, it's actually a rigid with a stainless electrics box sitting in the space where, on another frame, the rear shock would be. You'll ◗

The battery was sat on the bench when grinding sparks ignited the gases coming out of the venting breather and blew the top clean off!

2009
Nov 26

ISSUE
123

OTHER BIKES FEATURED:
Sportster bobber, V-Max, Bandit streetfighter

TINWARE:

Unknown front mudguard with stainless brackets by owner, modified King Sportster fuel tank, 6mm neoprene pads on steel base as seat, rear 'guard integral with frame, one-off stainless electrics/battery box stainless by owner

ELECTRICS:

Minimal main loom by owner, 4" Bates replica headlight, one-off tail-light by owner

PAINT:

Laverda metallic silver by owner

POLISHING:

Owner

ENGINEERING:

Owner

THANKS TO:

'Mark at Manic Motorcycles (01406 540775); Ginge at GLF Motorcycles (01775 761162); Andy Barber for donating the front calipers; & Jo for putting up with my tantrums when things didn't go to plan ...'

have noticed that it's been cleverly constructed to use the engine as a stressed member, in the same way the race boys at Harris and Spondon did with their famous frames, and you can't have failed to notice that ... umm ... 'individual' seat? Well, not unless you're actually physically blind anyway ... and, if that's the case, how are you reading this? We'll talk more about that in a moment (the seat that is, not your miraculous recovery from blindness), anyway, where did we get to?

Oh yeah, I remember. Yeah, while the frame may have been reasonably straightforward, the exhaust, Andy says, really wasn't – 'a pain in the arse' is how he describes it. It's been made by welding together fifty six

The exhaust was made by welding together fifty six individual bends and bits of tube.

individual bends and bits of tube and it all hangs off the front of the motor because there was nowhere else to mount it. Does look good, though, doesn't it? All sinuous and swoopy down there ...

With the frame built and the bike up on its wheels, attention could now be turned to the hundred and one other jobs that need to be done to turn a frame/engine/wheels into a fully functioning motorbike. One of the bigger jobs was the tank – he'd picked up a King Sportster, but it didn't look

quite right. He cut it in half and widened it at the front and stretched and narrowed it at the rear.

Mind you, he says that the rest of the build wasn't too bad – something that was helped by the fact that the firm he works for let him scavenge in their scrap bins for alloy and use their lathes in his own time. Because of this he was able to knock up bits like the handlebar grips, the footpegs and the controls among other things.

But just when he thought the hard work was all over, he says, the last two weeks of the build were just one problem after another. It took him days to get the

brakes and clutch bled and then he fucked up not one, but two brand new batteries in just two days.

The seat, and the back mudguard, are integral with the frame and while most folk don't seem to even see the rear 'guard, everyone, but everyone, remarks on the seat. Very reminiscent of the spinal column and vertebrae of something huge and ancient you'd see in the Natural History Museum, it's covered in 6mm thick neoprene pads to give it even some semblance of padding for your arse. Does it work? Dunno, you'd have to ask Andy, but he rode it to the Farmyard for its first outing and he wasn't walking as though he and Jo'd had a row and she'd rammed something hard and unyielding up his ... yes, well, you get my meaning.

Since then it's won two 'Best Engineering' trophies and also a 'Best Streetfighter' trophy and, he says, while he didn't build it to win trophies it is nice when others appreciate your work. The bike does pretty much what he wants it to with his only gripe being that, if you throw it into a roundabout too hard, you ground the exhaust out as it's so low but, apart from that, it's great to ride and he love it to bits. ✪

2010
Mar 18

ISSUE
127

OTHER BIKES FEATURED:
XV125 chop, Dutch Triumph, Sportster bobber

THE
SHADOW

WE'VE HAD A FEW HARLEYS ON THE COVER OF LATE SO, TO REDRESS THE BALANCE, HOW'S THIS? THE BEST-LOOKING HONDA SHADOW YOU'VE EVER SEEN OR WHAT?

PICS: **NIK** WORDS: **JOHN BRANDWOOD** MODEL: **MICHELLE MONROE (WWW.MICHELLE-MONROE.CO.UK)**

Alec Sharp, the bloke who built, but no longer owns, this really rather stunning VT600 Shadow chop was just twenty one when he built it. He'd been into custom bikes for years and had built a 125 Kawasaki chop that, he laughs, 'was cobbled together with massive rake and apes ... it was completely unrideable, but cool!'

At the time he was working on a farm in his native Suffolk, having done a part time welding course and another on bodywork, but then was fortunate enough to meet Clive from So Low Choppers and was given a job working there. After he'd been working at So Low and being involved with making bikes for around six months, he decided he was ready to have a serious go at building a bike so he stripped his perfectly good VT600 and started on the frame. He had, he says, a rough idea of what he wanted, but he likes the 'Chica' style of designing – allowing the bike to just develop naturally of its own accord.

Using his own ideas, but drawing off the font of all chopperdom knowledge that is Clive, he created a twin

He lost count of the days he spent locked in the container out the back of So Low Choppers, filling and rubbing down, filling and rubbing down the moulding.

downtube lowriding rigid from inch and an quarter CDS tube that cleverly cradles the water-cooled 'Onda's radiator between the front rails to keep the motor clean and free of what could've been unsightly water pumps and wossnames. Said radiator

has been fitted with an almost Rolls-Roycesque cover, or at least one with a distinct nod towards the days of the great British touring cars of yore, and so actually adds to the overall look of the bike as opposed to detracts from it as radiators can so easily do.

The plan had always been to re-use as much of the original bike as possible because he didn't want to spend pots of money on the project so the stock front and back ends of the Shadow have been used almost in their entirety. The ◐

SPEC SHEET

ORIGINAL YEAR, MAKE & MODEL:
1994 Honda VT600 Shadow

ENGINE:
1994 Honda VT600 Shadow, single 1.75" SU, one-off custom made manifold, alloy bell-mouth air-filter with mesh, one-off handmade 'pipes wrapped in black exhaust wrap

FRAME:
One-off handmade hardtail lowrider in 1.25" CDS tube, twin downtube, 35 degrees rake, 3.5" ground clearance

SHARP END:
1994 Honda VT600 Shadow wheel/brake/forks/yokes/master-cylinder, braided stainless steel brake lines, one-off handmade drag 'bars, microswitch switches, electronic speedo

BLUNT END:
1994 Honda VT600 Shadow wheel & brake, one-off handmade twisted bar torque arm

TINWARE:
Modified Midwest Motorcycle Supply Pro Image 2 tank with hand scalloped sides, Midwest Motorcycle Supply single seat, one-off handmade rear mudguard with hand scalloped sides, one-off handmade battery box

ELECTRICS:
Handmade one-off loom, Midwest Motorcycle Supply peaked headlight, honeycomb catseye tail-light, all electrics inside dummy oil tank (removed battery tray in rear of tank & plated in) including ignition & starter button

2010
Mar 18

ISSUE
127

OTHER BIKES FEATURED:
XV125 chop, Dutch Triumph, Sportster bobber

PAINT:

Black base with blue/ green translucent flake & scalloped panels in old English cream with baby blue pinstriping by owner & master painter/ craftsman Mr. Clive Ransome & Hilary of Hurricane Airbrush Art (07799 242721)

POWDER COATING:

Brackets/number plate holder/'bars/ battery holder/ parts of forward controls in satin black & wheels chrome powdercoated by Aerocoat (01493 488455 or 01493 488456 or www. aerocoat.net)

POLISHING:

Heads, forks, yokes, sprocket, drum, linkages, forwards by Specalised Polishing Services (01842 762700 or www.sps4u.co.uk)

ENGINEERING:

Bell crank for rear brake, forward mounts, engine mounting brackets, bars, rear wheel spacing, frame etc by owner

THANKS TO:

'Most importantly, So Low Choppers (01359 253600 or www. solowchoppers.co.uk) & Clive for his infinite wisdom in chopper matters, Mark Bunning for help with the mess of wires I got myself in, Hilary for being nice to me when everyone else was (& still are!) horrible to me, & Jay Ransome for constructively criticising everything I made; & Martin for making me a stainless steel axle when I was desperate!'

front end, for example, uses the stock nineteen inch front wheel, the stock forks and, surprisingly, the stock yokes. I say 'surprisingly' because, as any fule nose, most stock yokes are generally more unappealing to the eye than a dead mouse in a doner kebab but, looking at Alec's bike, they're not immediately visible as being stock ... if you see what I mean. It's probably down to the fact that as they're from a 'custom' bike, albeit a factory one, the yokes aren't quite as ugly as some, and the simplicity of the whole front end – with its little Z-bars with off-white grips and the large Midwest Motorcycle Supply headlight – overall.

In fact, it's this overall simplicity that makes the bike stand out. Alec's very much worked to the 'less is more' ethos. The thing, as anyone who's built bikes will know, getting a 'simple' bike is actually an extremely complicated affair – bikes are, by their very nature, complex things and paring on down to this level takes a hell of a lot more work than might at first meet the eye. Take the fuel tank, for example – it's a Midwest Motorcycle Supply Pro Image 2 tank which, in itself, is a very nice tank, but it wasn't quite right in Alec's eyes. Aware of trends on custom bike building and, as has been previously mentioned, influenced by the likes of Chica, he decided that the sides of his tank needed to be scalloped. Alec, though, wasn't quite happy with the

shape and so he re-worked the panels on So Low's English wheel, reshaped them and then welded them back in. The finished thing makes up for all the hard work and really suits the bike in a way that perhaps a stock aftermarket tank just wouldn't have done.

Of course, using a tank like this, and a rigid frame too obviously, meant that the stock Honda carb would no longer fit in the vee of the motor. That problem was solved by the use of an inch and three quarter

He'd previously cobbled together a 125 Kawasaki chop with massive rake and apes ... it was completely unrideable, but cool!

||||||||||||||||||||||||||||||||||||||||||||||||||||||||||||||||||||||||||

SU mounted on a one-off inlet manifold which, again, adds to the olde-worlde look of the whole build. Those little black-wrapped 'pipes do a similar job as does the little fake oil tank that's actually the battery/electrics box, the minimal rear mudguard and, of course, the simple little single seat which, unusually these days, doesn't have springs underneath it and looks all the better for it.

Juts about everything on the bike has been, Alec says, either were made from scratch or bought and modified and, after many, many nights and Sundays, he finally had her ready to paint ... or what he thought was ready to paint anyway. It turned out that, to get what he wanted, involved the whole frame being entirely moulded (as were the oil tank and the fuel tank). He says he lost count of the days he spent locked in the container out the back of So Low Choppers, filling and rubbing down, filling and rubbing down, but the end result was, I'm glad to say, amazing - once the paint and 'flake went on and the lacquer hit the paint, the bike just lit up! It was a joint effort by Alec and Clive – the black base with blue/green translucent flake and scalloped panels in old English cream – while the baby blue pinstriping was done by Hilary of Hurricane

Airbrush Art, So Low's in-house painter.

Final assembly, he reports, went real well after Clive had, thankfully, let him have a few days off to complete the bike as he was itching to get it on the road. The first start up was a little daunting as he was dubious about the SU working properly but, to his amazement, she fired up straight away and sounded nearly like a Big Twin, certainly bigger than 600cc! She is, he says 'super comfortable to ride ... well, for the first couple of miles anyway - after that your arse gradually works its way up to your ears!' ⊗

2010
June 10

ISSUE
130

OTHER BIKES FEATURED:
VN1500, Triumph chop, Replica Zephyr

LAST MINUTE WONDER

WORDS: GUY 'ELVIS' SIMONS
PICS: JOHN BRANDWOOD
MODEL: BECKY JO HAYHURST

SOMETIMES LEAVING EVERYTHING UNTIL THE LAST MINUTE MEANS THAT YOU WORK THAT BIT HARDER TO GET YOUR BIKE JUST RIGHT ...

Well, it does as far as I'm concerned - this is becoming somewhat of a recurring theme with me. You know how it is, there's loads to do but you keep telling yourself, 'there's ages yet, I'll do that next week'. Then wallop! Before you know it, your deadline's suddenly less than a month away and you've still got loads to do ... arrgh!

My deadlines always seem to be centred around our local bike fest - the famous Barton Bike Night - and the Faro Rally in Portugal. This was definitely the case in 2008 when my trike underwent a heart transplant six hours before departing for Plymouth on a 2500 mile

I loaded her up, 1.30am, job done – a whole seven hours to spare!

journey to Faro. On returning from it, which was trouble-free I hasten to add, I'd made my mind up - time to ditch the stabilisers and get a proper big boy's bike.

A plan was hatched with our fearless leader 'Buzz the Lightyear Barley' (aka Shaun) of Barley Custom Cycles, and a donor bike was soon purchased - a surprisingly nice 2000 Dyna 1450 for just £3000.

Within hours of getting home we decided to try the motor (the only bit we actually used in the end) - the damn thing wouldn't start or even try to. Two hours later we discovered some thieving git had robbed the timing chain! Ahhh, that'll be the problem then, eh? New chain on and pop, bang, fart and away she went - it lives! Shaun's next comment was 'right, rip it to bits'. Elliot (Shaun's son and general pain in the arse) was put to the task and a 'phone call soon followed, 'come and collect this heap of scrap'. So, armed with my camera, an eBay frenzy soon followed and the grand sum of £2795.63 clawed back. Woohoo, we do love our on-line auction site - a 2000 Twin Cam A engine that cost £204.37. Don't you just love it ◗

SPEC SHEET

ENGINE:

Harley-Davidson Twin Cam A, 1550 barrels & pistons, Arlen Ness air-filter, Screamin' Eagle ignition, one-off stainless exhaust by Shaun Barley, one-off jackshaft by Shaun Barley

FRAME:

One-off by Shaun Barley, modified SMT Engineering foot controls & rests

SHARP END:

80 spoke 18x4" wheel, Suzuki Bandit wavy disc, Suzuki GSX-R caliper, 60mm CDS inverted springers by Shaun Barley, one-off 3" billet yokes by Shaun Barley, one-off 50mm CDS handlebars by Shaun Barley with one-off internal twist grip throttle & clutch, SMT Engineering master-cylinders, Demon Cycles 50mm digital speedo

BLUNT END:

One-off swingarm by Shaun Barley, Demon Cycles Slim Line softail shocks, 80 spoke 17x12" wheel, 330 tyre, Demon Cycles sprocket brake, 1.5" over stock belt, 132 tooth pulley

2010
June 10

ISSUE
130

OTHER BIKES FEATURED:
VN1500, Triumph chop, Replica Zephyr

TINWARE:

One-off hand made alloy fuel tank, one-off hand made seat with Smart Rrrs (01347 811978 or www.smartrrrs.biz) cover, one-off side panels moulded into frame

ELECTRICS:

One-off loom by Shaun Barley, Eyeball headlight, Demon Cycles' LED tail light

PAINT:

Matt white by Elliott Barley

POLISHING:

Elliott Barley

ENGINEERING:

Designed by owner & Shaun & Elliott Barley, engineered by Shaun & Elliott

THANKS TO:

'Shaun & Elliott Barley at Barley Custom Cycles (shaunbarley@aol com) for everything; Mansfield Anodisers (01623 627700 or www.mansfield-anodisers.co.uk); Wendy for bringing supplies; & my dad for letting me skive off work ..'

An eBay frenzy soon followed and the grand sum of £2795.63 clawed back. Woohoo, - a 2000 Twin Cam A engine that cost £204.37.

when a plan comes together?

The build began December '08. The front hoop was fabricated in a matter of hours and the engine mounts completed, then other projects and real paying customers started requesting Shaun's specialist services. That was okay, there was no rush - my chop didn't need to be done 'til July, that's seven months away, loads of time yet! Still, I was purchasing parts from our friends in the States and soon had all the bits we required including a 17x12" 80 spoke rear wheel and an 18x4" front to match. Then a call to Demons Cycle (www.demonscycle.com) secured most of the other parts – sprocket brake, billet shocks and the all-important internal clutch and throttle assembles. The search for forwards with

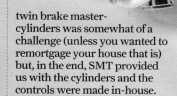

twin brake master-cylinders was somewhat of a challenge (unless you wanted to remortgage your house that is) but, in the end, SMT provided us with the cylinders and the controls were made in-house.

Works began again around Easter 2009. No worries, that's a massive twelve weeks until Barton Bike Night. The aim was to keep things clean and simple - the rear end was soon constructed along with the jack-shaft, the seat unit and swingarm, and the suspension geometry was then worked out with a sophisticated piece of equipment which Shaun created himself comprising of a Quality Street tin lid, some wire and a piece of flat bar all held together Blue Peter style. It worked though. Not much to do now, we thought, we'd easily make the deadline and

there was even talk of making the Farmyard for a dummy run. I mean, front end, tank and few wires? How long's that gunna take?

The bike was always going to have a springer-type front

sourced locally (very locally) and the owner relieved of it ... if you get what I mean. We got One-Eyed Scotch Billy to check the alignment and, with that sorted, it was time to strip the bike down and concentrate on paint and nice bits.

Time was ticking by, though, and there was no time to wait for unreliable chromers so anodising was the way forward - thanks to the boys at Mansfield Anodising for the speedy turn-around and an excellent job. Elliot set to work as chief moulder and prep man ... just four weeks from 'D-day'. The big decision now was 'what colour?' It came to me in a drunken moment with a can of Carling in my hand - black and white and made with 100% British Barley'. Perfect! So matt white and black was the order. Late one Sunday night Shaun painted the complete bike with matt white. Monday morning came and I received a 'phone call, 'You know this matt finish you wanted? I can see my reflection in it!' Oh shit! The paint supplier had mixed it wrong. With that issue re-solved we began the rebuilding process with only 10 days to the deadline.

This part of the build wasn't too bad - a few late nights (and earache from the missus), but soon there she was all built up, wired up, fuelled up and ready to roll. Surprisingly, she fired up first try – finally, things seemed to be going our way. We did a couple of short runs to iron out any teething problems (such as cables stretching and finding the bits we'd forgotten ❍

end, but not as you see here. The original plan was Olhins shocks on the front of the legs but, since then I'd found some bargain Bandit wavy discs, when the shockers were offered into place it looked all wrong. So billet shocks to match the rear were deemed needed, but even that wasn't that simple - the springs were so hard they would've shaken my fillings out. Shaun cannibalised a set of standard Harley legs for some softer springs ... and it worked. Bouncy bouncy.

The front suspension linkage was a point of discussion for many a late night with both Shaun and myself conducting late night sketching sessions trying to figure out how to get bearings to fit and work. Having had experience with other springer front ends, floppy bushes just were not going to suffice - taper bearings all round for this bad boy. Shaun then knocked up a set of slabs out of some 3" billet with radiused edges - sweet.

At this point our attention turned toward the tank. It had to be big enough for 4.5 gallons of fuel, but still be in keeping with the clean and simple lines of the bike. Shaun just knocked this one up quickly, as he does, and that was it - the finished thing. Well, sort of ...

I still had no handlebars, so some 50mm tubing was ✪

2010
June 10

ISSUE
130

OTHER BIKES FEATURED:
VN1500, Triumph chop, Replica Zephyr

118 LEGENDS THE VERY BEST CUSTOM BIKES
FROM THE PAGES OF 100% BIKER

The Moto Club Faro Rally 2009 was the debut for my matt white vision and we picked up Second Chop in the custom show so all the trouble was definitely worth it.

to Loctite). By this time it was 24 hours to Barton Bike Night so Elliott and I set off on a 100 mile test ride down the M180 and back at full chat ... it pissed down all the way. Oh well, tested the electrics at least. We'd done it with hours to spare! At Barton, wow, what a response we got (most people asked when it was going to be out of primer ... cheeky sods).

Over the next couple of days, a few more miles were put under the wheels and a luggage rack made, all ready for the 3500 mile trip to Faro and back. The weekend on which we were due to leave came and I took the bike home on the Friday evening to load up for the early morning start for Plymouth Saturday. I was so relieved that, finally, my dream had come true but, just as I rolled onto my drive, the headlight fell off. Into the garage and four hours later I'd rustled up a temporary replacement out of some scrap from behind the shed. I loaded her up, 1.30am, job done – a whole seven hours to spare!

At 6.30 this next morning I had a flat battery and a leaking fuel tap. I was about ready to throw the towel in and take my BMW, but the missus stepped in and assured me that Shaun would sort it (as he always does) and, once I'd got it to his workshop, he did. So that was it – away we went. The Moto Club Faro Rally 2009 was the debut for my matt white vision and we picked up Second Chop in the custom show so all the trouble was definitely worth it. No major issues to report on route either – slight oil leak, snapped clutch cable and, oh yeah, lost the suicide shift at 90mph racing to the port but, hey, wouldn't be as much fun if nothing occurred, would it?

As with all the bikes out of the Barley Custom Cycles stable, they are built to be ridden and used and abused in all weathers, but we still get the same comments - 'you can't ride that far' or 'it won't go round corners', but the favourite is always 'I bet that came on a trailer'. How wrong can they be! If a bike can't be ridden 400 miles in a day then it's not a bike, it's an ornament.

So we'll see what 2010 brings. I haven't got any plans to change it, just to use it so keep an eye out at the rallies. Maybe there'll be a new project for 2011, we'll see – there's loads of time yet, isn't there? ✪

STRIKE TRUE II

STRIKE TRUE II, BUILT BY SHAW HARLEY-DAVIDSON IN EAST SUSSEX, TOOK TOP HONOURS AT THE RECENT AMD ROUND AT ALLY PALLY AND WON A PLACE IN THE WORLD CHAMPIONSHIPS OF CUSTOM BIKE BUILDING IN STURGIS.

WORDS: NIK **PICS:** ASA INFINITY STUDIOS **MODEL:** MONICA HARRIS

It belongs to a gentleman by the name of Shaun and is the second bike he's had built with the Strike True moniker. The name 'Strike True' refers to the RAF Bomber Command's motto in World War II – 'Strike Hard, Strike Sure' – and was chosen in memory of his grandfather.

The bike was inspired by a mix of things. He wanted a bike that had a vintage racer

It had to look like it was doing 100mph even when it was standing still.

|||||||||||||||||||||||||||||||||||||||||

feel to it – it had be low-slung and look, to paraphrase the legendary Edward Turner (even though he was talking about Triumphs), like it was doing 100mph even when it was standing still. He'd seen Krugger Motorcycles' 'Racer' too and liked the overall stance of it but, as with all custom builds, there were things about it he'd've changed if it were his, and so he took what he liked about it and integrated it into the new project. The ◗

SPEC SHEET

ORIGINAL YEAR, MAKE & MODEL:
2009 Harley-Davidson FLSTSB Crossbones

ENGINE:
2009 Harley-Davidson FLSTSB Crossbones, 96 cubic inch (1584cc), Garage 65 air-filter, Vance & Hines Competition 'pipes, braided stainless oil lines, Roland Sands Design rocker covers/ timing cover/derby cover, Performance Machine starter cover/ transmission cover

FRAME:
2009 Harley-Davidson FLSTSB Crossbones, cleaned up & smoothed, Performance Machine forwards with Chops 76 brass 'pegs

SHARP END:
21" Harley-Davidson wheel/disc, Performance Machine caliper/master-cylinders/controls/ switches, Goodridge brake line, Paughco 2" under springers, 1940 Speedster 'bars, internal throttle, Chops 76 brass grips

BLUNT END:
Modified stock swingarm with sprocket disc conversion by Shaw Speed & Custom, lowered stock shocks, 17" Harley-Davidson wheel, Performance Machine caliper, side-mount numberplate

2010
July 8

ISSUE
131

OTHER BIKES FEATURED:
Trike supplement, GN250 Suzuki, Softail Harley

The brass tank-retaining strip both keeps the tank down and, again, adds to the vintage feel of the whole project.

||||||||||||||||||||||||||||||||||||||||||||||||||||||||||||||||||||||||||||||||||||||||||||||||||

TINWARE:
One-off alloy front number plate by Shaw Speed & Custom, modified H-D tank with integral digital speedo & brass centre console by Shaw's Speed & Custom, Roland Sands Design seat re-covered by Saxon Seats, one-off rear mudguard by Shaw Speed & Custom, New York City Choppers oil tank

ELECTRICS:
Modified stock loom, Crime Scene Choppers headlight & tail light, LED H-D indicators, coil re-located under tank, voltage regulator re-located under engine, re-located ignition switch

PAINT:
Vintage pale blue by Image Design Custom

POLISHING:
Image Design Custom

ENGINEERING:
Shaw Speed & Custom (01825 872003 or www.shawharley-davidson.co.uk)

THANKS TO:
'Image Design Custom Paint (01276 709319 or www.imagedesign custom.co.uk)'

other design briefs were that the engine parts had to be powdercoated black, there had to be some brass used (again, to give that olde-worlde nod to the past) and the bike was to be as clean as possible in terms of wiring, lines and layout.

It was decided that a Softail Crossbones was the ideal base to start from

and so one was sourced and the project began. Firstly, the bike was totally stripped and the frame had its welds smoothed and cleaned, while the swingarm was modified to take a caliper on the nearside to allow Neil, Shaw Speed & Custom's custom technician, to move both the sprocket and the braking assembly all to the one side to give a really clean look to the right hand side of the motorcycle.

The next job was the fuel tank. After spending what probably felt like an eternity choosing a tank to start cutting up, and taking

style cues from the Krugger bike, Shaw's fabricating genius Dave Rollison sculpted the tank so that it sat just so on the frame – as low as was humanly possible, with little cut-outs to allow the engine's rocker covers to not be obscured by the lower edge of the tank. He also made the brass tank-retaining strip that both keeps the tank down and, again, adds to the vintage feel of the whole project, and set a digital speedo in the left hand dummy fuel cap where the fuel gauge used to live.

A two inch under front end was ordered from Paughco and stripped ready to be painted, and a new bracket was welded to the nearside leg to allow the fitting of a racing number board that would both clean up the look of the front end and also be an essential part of the overall style.

The rear mudguard, although looking a simple and straightforward design, was actually one of the components that took the longest. It

needed to be short and sit close to the tyre - something which, you would have thought, wouldn't be that difficult a thing to source ... In reality, however, after hours and hours and hours of offering up mudguard after mudguard after mudguard, walking away, squinting at them and then rejecting them, they decided that no steel 'guard, no matter how they modified it, would be quite right and so the best way to sort it would be to make a new one up in fibreglass. To give the look and feel of metal, though, a layer of aluminium was added to the mould and now most onlookers are unaware that it's anything but.

Finally, a new oil tank was ordered from New York City Choppers and fitted in the frame in the space where the stock one once lived, and the coil and regulator were also relocated up under the tank and under the engine respectively to clean up the look of the motor. ◗

2010
July 8

ISSUE
131

OTHER BIKES FEATURED:
Trike supplement, GN250 Suzuki, Softail Harley

The rear mudguard was actually one of the components that took the longest

IIIIIIIIIIIIIIIIIIIIIIIIIIIIIIIIIIIIIIIIIIIIIIIIIIIIIIIIIIIIIIIIIIIIIIIIIIIIIIIIIIIIIIIIIIIIIIIIIIIIIIIIIIIIIIIIIIIIIIIIIIIIIIIIIIIIIIIIIIIIIIIII

With all parts modified and prepared, the frame and all the tins (as our American cousins would say), and the modified 1940 Speedster handlebars, were taken to Image Design Custom in Camberley in Surrey to be prepped ready for the vintage pale blue paintscheme.

After receiving all the parts back reassembly took place - the wheels were rebuilt with the newly devised sprocket and rotor assembly, and the Speedster 'bars were fitted with up to date Performance Machine hydraulic clutch and brake master-cylinders and switchgear, complimented with Chops 76 brass handlebar grips and an internal throttle to give a clean handlebar set-up. The tank was fitted with its polished sides and gold leaf decals, and a Roland Sands Design seat kit was used with a Shaw's aluminium battery cover and the seat was covered with leather and carved with the 'Strike II' legend. The engine was dressed with a mixture of Roland Sands Designs and Performance Machine covers, a stunning

brass and glass Garage 65 (the Italian custom shop who built the Ally Pally winning KCosmodrive) air filter and a set of stainless Vance & Hines Competition 'pipes that have been de-shined for, again, that modern vintage look ... if you see what I mean.

PM forwards were fitted along with brass 'pegs and brake and clutch pedals, again to give a traditional feel, and that brass theme is continued by the covers on the low-mounted Crime Scene Choppers head and tail lights (the latter side-mounted on the left). The number 13 decals were added, along with the small, round LED indicators, and that, for all effects and purposes, was that – 'Strike True II' was finished.

The bike then went on to Ally Pally in February for the Ace Cafe custom bike show and won the modified Harley-Davidson category, and the second Best In Show prize too - winning a place at the AMD World Championship final in Sturgis in America in August. It then went to Frankfurt for the Custom Chrome Show in March where they were hosting the European Championships and it gained a very creditable fourth place in a heavily competitive arena. Shaun, it's reported, is more than pleased with how his bike has come out and, now that the weather's improved, is looking forward to getting some miles under its wheels. ✪

2010
Aug 5

ISSUE
132

OTHER BIKES FEATURED:
USA customs supplement, V Max chop, Bourneville café racer

THE MANTIS

AT ALLY PALLY EARLIER THIS YEAR ONE OF THE BIKES WITH A CONSTANT CROWD OF PEOPLE AROUND IT WAS THIS – TONY BUCKINGHAM'S 'THE MANTIS'. THEY DON'T COME MUCH MORE IN-YER-FACE THAN THIS!

WORDS: TONY 'BUCK' BUCKINGHAM **PICS:** ASA INFINITY STUDIOS
MODEL: LEANNE BUCKINGHAM

2010
Aug 5

ISSUE
132

OTHER BIKES FEATURED:
USA customs supplement, V Max chop, Bourneville café racer

several years ago, I had a hankering to build a bike that was beautiful but had a sinister look about it, all tied in with a splash of Stateside '70s excess. Something themed on, say, the creature from the movie 'Alien' was just the sorta thing I had in mind, but it'd been done a few times already and, with a couple of great examples already to be seen here in the UK, I thought 'naw' and left the idea to simmer away in the background.

One night around three years ago while watching TV and channel hopping through all the repeats, I dropped onto a nature programme all about ... yeah, you guessed it ... the praying mantis and wham! I had a flash of inspiration moment! Here was the creature I was looking for to use as the theme of my bike and, after taking in

The idea behind it was that I wasn't trying to make an actual mantis, but a bike that had a mantis feel about it.

the rest of the documentary, I went over to my PC and, once my porn had finished downloading (ahem), I went into research mode looking at pics of the little monster ... the mantis, I mean, we're not talking about porn now. I drew up a few doodles of how I saw the bike and eventually finished with a picture I was happy with - this was going to be my starting point and the inspiration to see me through the crap times ahead in the build and, boy, I did not realise how many there were to be!

The idea behind it was that I wasn't trying to make an actual mantis, but a bike that had a mantis feel about it. The 'bars and the long forks had to

give a feeling of the creature's antennae and front legs, and the lights had be positioned where they are, rather than conventionally, to give the impression of eyes. And, as you look around the bike, I wanted there to be other mantis-like areas too – the tank, for

example, had to be reminiscent of the insect's carapace – and, although they do come in other colours too, the most well-known colour for mantises is green so the bike's colour scheme was decided right at the beginning of the build. I also wanted it to be a rolling ○

SPEC SHEET

ENGINE:
Revtec 110 inch, polished, heads & barrels powdercoated candy green with diamond cutting edge effect, twin IDF dual throat carburettors with straight through air rams, Barnet Scorpion clutch, modified Ultima belt primary, Wontec RSD gearbox, Accel plugs, Revtec HT wire set, Accel coil, Daytona Twin Tec ignition, much modified custom exhausts, rubber oil lines covered with green layer then surrounded by stainless coil spring for effect

FRAME:
One-off rigid spoon style with 48 deg rake by Joe & Lucky Buck Custom Cycles, modified Accutronix forwards

SHARP END:
21" Xtreme wheel with 90 Metzeler tyre, modified custom built 10" over '70's Harman-style forks, one-off hand-made handlebars & throttle

REAR END:
18" Xtreme wheel & disc, 200 Metzeler tyre, Jaybrake caliper, one-off torque arm, Revtec nickel-plated chain, Xtreme sprocket, one-off chain jockey wheel

2010
Aug 5

ISSUE
132

OTHER BIKES FEATURED:
USA customs supplement, V Max chop, Bourneville café racer

BODYWORK:

Modified Paul Yaffe front mudguard with extra side barbs & hand cut relief pattern on top with raised flutes on top & side, very modified custom fuel tank, one-off seat by Lucky Buck Custom Cycles & Tealess' Trim Shop (01733 313 692 or www.tealesstrimshop. co.uk), very modified custom rear 'guard, all other panels custom made one-offs

ELECTRICS:

One-off main loom, Fred Kodlin billet headlights, Paul Yaffe tail light, green LED highlight strips hidden through out bike, Motorgadget digital speedo in one-off surround

PAINT:

Shades of candy green with colour changing fleck under the candy & movement flake on top, blending/prep/prime by Buck, base coats/ effect coats/clear by A&C Auto Refinishers (01353 675240 or www. acautorefinishers. co.uk), airbrushing by Air Art

POWDER COATING:

Heads & barrels by Sumax

POLISHING/ PLATING:

Chrome & 22ct gold plate & polishing by JD Wyatt (01842 766770), polishing by Lucky Buck Custom Cycles, engraving by Degs

ENGINEERING:

All work done in-house by Lucky Buck Custom Cycles (01353 86133 or www. luckybuckcustoms.com)

THANKS TO:

'Will; Ron; Joe; Woz; Degs; Paul; John; & the guys at Custom Chrome ...'

right – the barbs everywhere on the bike mirror the ones on the actual creature. The design called for the bike to look just so and that's made it a very complex machine - many parts have been sited not for ease or efficiency, but for aesthetics and doing this brought along a sea of challenges with it as well.

For example, it's fine hanging the battery under the bike and shoe-horning most of the electrics in there too, but it's a bloody bitch to work on after the build. The fuel pipe runs down the inside of the frame to the fuel pump, back in and up the frame to the carbs - all to save six inches of plastic tube from

I overheard a woman at a show say, 'Oh my God, it's a mantis' while she was still twenty feet away

demonstration of just what my bike-building business, Lucky Buck Custom Cycles, could do if we put our minds to it and so only the best components were to be used and hang the expense ... well, sort of, anyway, he said wincing at the thought of how much it cost.

Anyway, the start of the build was the purchase of a 110 cubic inch (1800 approx cc) Revtech engine with a Wontec right side

drive gearbox. Joe, my frame-building genius, then set about hand-making a suitable frame for them – a high headstock rigid with forty eight degrees of rake and an eighteen inch rear wheel with a 200 tyre. The very '70s Harman-style forks were ordered from the States and then modified here at Lucky Buck until they sat just how I wanted them, and they're fitted, at one end, with a brakeless 21" Xtreme matching wheel and, at the other, a set of 'bars made in-house with hours of work gone into the barbs and making everything blend in as a whole. The same applies to all of the bodywork too – the fuel tank actually started life as a common or garden custom tank until we cut the hell out of it and re-shaped it to look like the upper body of the mantis, and the front and rear mudguards and the chin spoiler took an equal amount of work to get just

being visible. All the wires also run inside the frame tubes and so that means that now that the backbone is as full as a porn actress with a donkey (and I should know, I have the movie)!

The damn thing fought me all the way too. Just one example was me spending two whole days f'king around with a speedo module surround, just to come to the conclusion it looked wrong and didn't work for me. After seventeen hours in the shop that day, I was so pissed off that I just threw the damn thing at the wall ... only for it to bounce straight through a window nearby. That cost another £50 to put right, and I cut my hand on the glass too, just to finish what had been a really stinking day. Mind you, it wasn't helped by outside influences taking the piss too - Customs & Excise did their bid to help my stress level rise after I'd stripped the heads and barrels and sent them off to the States for, firstly, powder coating and, secondly, to have the fins diamond cut. I'd filled in all the correct forms and sent them off and so it should've all gone straightforwardly but, on the return of the parts, the bastards wanted to bill me import charges and VAT based on the value they had been insured for, plus the work I'd had done. After a very restrained chat with the woman from C&E I nearly lost the plot when she just couldn't get her head around the fact that these items already belonged to me in the first instance, that I'd already paid VAT on them once, and that I was only sending them to have a decorative finish applied. After hours and hours and hours on the 'phone at different times with different staff, they finally waived the VAT but still charged me to import my own property back into the UK!

With all the fabrication done, it was time for paint and polish. JD Wyatt's in

Thetford took care of plating and polishing all the parts that needed to made shiny, including the stuff that had been engraved by Degs. They also did the 22 carat gold highlights too. I mixed up the blend of paint I wanted and prepped and primed everything ready for A&C Auto Finishers to lay down the base coats and add the effects (there's a change-colour fleck under the candy green and a 'movement' flake over the top of it). Air Air airbrushed in all the insect-like plates and such, and then A&C drowned it all in clear coat and polished it until it was feet deep. Assembling it again after all this was the usual nightmare of desperately trying not to scratch anything and I was very relieved when ◗

2010
Aug 5

ISSUE
132

OTHER BIKES FEATURED:
USA customs supplement, V Max chop, Bourneville café racer

MANTIS

132 LEGENDS THE VERY BEST CUSTOM BIKES
FROM THE PAGES OF 100% BIKER

it was all back together and in one undamaged piece.

So, the big question, how does it ride? Well, let me ask you this – can you pat yourself on the head while rubbing circles on your stomach at the same time? Yes? Well then, you should find riding it a piece of piss - you'll easily get the hang of the left foot clutch and the left hand shift with twist transmission brake, and the conventional throttle and rear brake. If not then, well, you won't. That's about the long and short of it ...

Wherever I take the bike, it's the centre of attention and has already brought in work for the shop so, I s'pose, that's the reason I built it (along with the fact that, basically, I could) justified. I overheard a woman at a show say, 'Oh my God, it's a mantis' while she was still twenty feet away so I asked her what made her think that and she replied, 'I lived abroad where the creature lives and one day one dropped from a bush onto my shoulder. I turned and looked into its eyes from about two inches away - trust

The fuel tank actually started life as a common or garden custom tank until we cut the hell out of it and re-shaped it to look like the upper body of the mantis.

me, you've got it spot on!'

Is it for sale? Well, maybe. I intend to keep it for two or three years and display it as part of my on-going promotion of my bike building business. However, if someone came along with a sensible offer, I may just let it go. I've already been had a rock band, some kind of insect hotel (or something?) and an adult magazine enquire about using it in photo shoots. Life rolls on, though, and just off the ramps is a GSX1400 trike (that's just been shot by Trike magazine), and we're doing a Pro-Street Sportster and an ol' skool bobber with fatbobs, hand change and a girder front end – normal bikes, if you like. It's nice to do these and not have to think about insects for a while, I can tell you ... in fact, after three years building this bike, I can tell you that I don't think I EVER wanna see another bug as long as I live! ✪

2010
Sept 2

ISSUE
133

OTHER BIKES FEATURED:
Budget Suzuki, Aprilia café racer, V Rod

THE GENUINE ARTICLE!

LADIES AND GENTLEMEN, THE VEHICLE IN FRONT OF YOU IS THE REAL DEAL – THE ONE AND ONLY GENUINE EXILE TRIKE (WITH A CAPITAL T AS IT'S ITS NAME) IN EUROPE.

WORDS: NIK **PICS:** ASA INFINITY STUDIOS **MODEL:** LUCY-ANN BROOKS

There are, as far as we know, only three Exile Trikes actually in existence – the one that Russell Mitchell built for the original Biker Build-Off TV programme, another one for he did for someone else, and this one here which belongs to a gentleman by the name by the name of Paul Fenton from Royston in Herts.

He's the man behind BXtreme Customs – a company set up a few years ago to build custom bikes and trikes in conjunction with Exile Cycles, Battistinis and Richard Millard of Tattoos Optional (Skullchoppa). The combination of all these folk means that there are years of experience behind every build they undertake, and that they can use the best parts on the market including

Arlen Ness, Roland Sands, Leroy Thompson, Westbury handcrafted motorcycle parts and Drag Specialties. BXtreme also sells those parts too.

He set up his company after, he says, a life changing illness – taking the bull by the horns, he sold his home, bought a motor-home and an enclosed bike trailer and went on the road selling parts to the public direct – something he was able to do at good prices because his overheads are a lot lower than other shops. He fell in love with the Exile Trike after seeing it on the Biker Build-Off (as did almost everyone I've ever met) and just had to have one and so, back in 2008, he bit the bullet and ordered one from the legendary Mr Mitchell and his Stateside crew. It arrived a few months later and was built up by Richard Millard –

that's right, built up. You see, much as you might imagine the Trike comes as just that – a trike - it doesn't, you have to build it from the parts that you buy. Yes, you can order one direct from Exile already built and running but (a) it's quite a bit more expensive to do so and (b) they're in America so the hassles of shipping a complete vehicle are much more extensive than shipping a crate full of parts ... obviously.

Paul's machine is built around a 124 cubic inch (a smidge over two litres!) Total Performance engine with a ◗

SPEC SHEET

ORIGINAL YEAR, MAKE & MODEL:

2008 Exile Cycles Trike

ENGINE:

Exile Cycles Trike Total Performance 124 cubic inch (just over 2 litre), Exile Cycles foot clutch, Primo 3" open belt kit, no motor plate, 0.75 inch pulley offset, Jim's six speed gearbox with grenade shifter, Tech Cycle 2.0kw starter, Exile Monster shot-gun style 'pipes in raw steel with polished billet tips

FRAME:

2008 Exile Cycles Trike, Exile Cycles forwards

SHARP END:

Exile Cycles Monster 21x3.5" wheel, 120 section Metzeler tyre, Exile brake, 8" over SJP Tech Glide 250 forks & yokes, Exile Cycles Fat Bar drag 'bars with integral risers/internal throttle/push button switches

---

It's almost the ultimate exercise in minimalism and it looks utterly stunning because of it.

2010
Sept 2

ISSUE
133

OTHER BIKES FEATURED:
Budget Suzuki, Aprilia café racer, V Rod

BLUNT END:

Exile Cycles Trike axle/diff/brakes, Exile Cycles 25.5x18" wheels, Goodyear Formula 1 tyres

TINWARE:

Exile Cycles Trike fuel tank with flush mount cap, Exile Cycles oil tank, Le Pera solo seat

ELECTRICS:

Battistinis EZ wiring harness, SJP 3.5" headlight, Lazer Star micro B tail-lights

PAINT:

Matt black by Exile Cycles

POLISHING:

Scotchbrite finish by Exile Cycles

ENGINEERING:

Exile Cycles

THANKS TO:

'Richard Millard from Skull Choppa for helping with the build (www.tattoosoptional. co.uk); Exile Cycles (www.exilecycles. com); Ania Gavel (www. massagedivision.com); Hawg Haven (www. hawghaven.co.uk); & the Hells Angels for their friendship & support ...'

Jim's six speed gearbox (with grenade shifter!) and a Primo three inch open belt primary, a Tech Cycle two kilowatt starter (they take some starting these gert big motors!) and, of course, a set of Exile Monster shotgun 'pipes that, to be honest, it really wouldn't have looked right without. The motor has, of course, been Scotchbrited to within an inch of its life because, as any fule nose, Exile doesn't really do shiny ...

The frame it sits in is a modified Daytec/Exile one that's been hooked up to a belt-driven diff that's made almost exclusively in-house at Exile. The axle set-up itself is very, very narrow – barely wide enough to allow the rider to sit between the two twenty five and a half inch wide eighteen inch solid wheels with their massive Goodyear Eagle tyres – and, like the motor, has also been Scotchbrited to remove any trace of shininess. There are no mudguards at either end, no clocks, no front brake, no visible cables – nothing to clutter the appearance of

the Trike whatsoever. There's nothing unnecessary either – the engine needs an exhaust and an oil tank so they're there; the fuel needs to be held somewhere so there's a tank that sits just so; the rider needs controls so there're a set of 'bars with everything hidden so that they look just like a set of 'bars, nothing more, nothing less, and a set of forwards with the same lack of clutter about them. Okay, so the seat's got a couple of springs, it has to be said, but if it didn't then the seat would

have to be mounted to the frame in some way that, I'm fairly sure, wouldn't be anywhere near as simple-looking – it's designed to be somewhere to park yer arse on, no fuss, no mither, and that's what you do on it. Similarly, the classic Exile paint scheme of matt or satin black with Scotchbrited alloy – yes, you could paint and polish the Trike and it would look fantastic, but it wouldn't have the same visual impact as the plain, no nonsense, in-yer-face look that's made Exile bikes so

famous. It's its simplicity that makes it stand out.

In fact, probably the best description of the Trike is that it looks like it shouldn't work – that it isn't finished – when, of course, it does and it is. You know when you're building a bike, or a trike, and you get the big lumps done and are left with your creation in bare metal before you start adding the bits that're needed to actually make it work, to make it into a bike? Well, that's what the Exile Trike looks like – the cleverness of its design is down to keeping that totally stripped look, but having a working machine. It's almost the ultimate exercise in minimalism and it looks utterly stunning because of it and, personally, I think it should

The motor has, of course, been Scotchbrited to within an inch of its life because, as any fule nose, Exile doesn't really do shiny ...

be up there with the all-time greats of design like the Fender Stratocaster, the Supermarine Spitfire, the Mercedes Benz 300SL or the E-Type Jaguar. It's spawned a host of imitators (my own trike included), but no one has yet equalled the original in my eyes.

Anyway, enough of my flannel! Paul's now had the Trike for a couple of years and it is his pride and joy.

At the 2009 Bulldog Bash

it won 'Best Bike Trike' and, as Russell Mitchell was there, Paul asked him if he would collect the award with him as a way of thanking him for all his support. He also showed it on the Exile stand at the Ally Pally custom show (which is where I saw it and started mothering him about photographing it) and at the Ace Cafe's Harley-Davidson evenings on the last Thursday of the month during the Summer. ✖

2010
Sept 30

ISSUE
134

OTHER BIKES FEATURED:
A7 Bobber, T120

HOT ROD

ROB, THE OWNER AND BUILDER OF THIS TRIUMPH 'HOT ROD' CHOP WAS BORN FORTY TO FIFTY YEARS TOO LATE IN THE WRONG COUNTRY AND ERA – HE'S A FIFTIES AND SIXTIES AMERICANA INFLUENCED KIND OF GUY.

WORDS: BOB **PICS:** ASA INFINITY STUDIOS
MODEL: ROSIE WHITEMAN (WWW.ROSIEWHITEMAN.CO.UK)

This is reflected in the kind of clothes he wears and the style of bikes that he builds and rides - his last was a pumped-up version of a café racer with a 1853cc Ultima motor, the one before a '50s influenced Harley bobber, and before that a '60s influenced chop again a V-twin. With this build, though, he decided to go with a Triumph twin motor for no better reason than he'd never built one and, more importantly, they look cool.

On calling his contacts nationwide and perusing that well known auction website it soon became apparent that the original Meriden-built period Triumph motor he was seeking was (a) rare and hard to find and, more importantly, (b) prohibitively expensive. With this in mind he sourced a 2006 Thruxton motor, carbs and electric pack from Sandy at Triumph'ant over in Wales. The Thruxton, at 865cc, was the biggest capacity twin that Triumph were producing at the time and for what Rob had in mind

The original Meriden-built period Triumph motor he was seeking was (a) rare and hard to find and, more importantly, (b) prohibitively expensive.

he figured it would be plenty big and powerful enough. He next purchased from Scooby a Harley wideglide front end and a pair of RST stainless brake discs. Next on his shopping list were some wheels and a frame - the wheels, both Harley and a 21" front and a 150x16 rear complete with tyres, were easily purchased on eBay, but the frame was a very different matter ... This was taken care of by two mates and fellow Chopper Club members – firstly, Johnny A fabbed the headstock

to suit the aforementioned wide glide front end, and then John at Wookey Custom Cycles in Williton did his usual top job of bending ◗

SPEC SHEET

ENGINE:

2006 Triumph Thruxton 900, carbs rejetted, one-off bellmouths by Larry, modified engine covers, 2" wrapped stainless one-off exhausts by owner, eBay oil cooler

FRAME:

One-off hardtail frame by Jon NCC Somerset (Wookey Customs 07775 911210), Suzuki Intruder sidestand, one-off oil cooler/ seat/miscellaneous brackets by owner

SHARP END:

Harley-Davidson wide glide front end with modified yokes, shaved fork legs, 21" Harley wheel, Nissin 4 pot caliper, Brembo brake set-up, RST disc, one-off Z-bars by owner

BLUNT END:

16" Harley-Davidson wheel, Nissin 2 pot caliper, Brembo brake set-up, one-off sprocket, RST disc

TINWARE:

Modified King Sportster tank, one-off seat, one-off ribbed rear mudguard

2010
Sept 30

ISSUE
134

OTHER BIKES FEATURED:
A7 Bobber, T120

and welding tubes together to form the tidy hardtail frame.

First job then was to sort mounts for everything so Rob made and fitted the axle plates and covers, the steering stop, the mounts for the battery box, oil cooler, petrol tank, seat, number plate, side stand, coil, solenoid, reg/rectifier and head steady for the top of the engine, and all was going well until it came to the tank. A purchase he'd made a while before and had stashed away for a project such as this, there was no way it was going to fit as it was so that left him two options - either the frame or the tank gets introduced to Mr. Angle Grinder or he gets another

To complete the front end his son James bought him period grips and fork gaiters for Christmas.

tank. Out came Mr. Grinder and he cut a recess into the top tube of his brand new frame, flattened it off and rewelded it, and now the tank sits just right.

Next up was the rear mudguard, another eBay purchase. This was cut and ground to the exact size and length and then ribbed, and he then fabbed a pair of struts to suit and Scotchbrited it back to bare metal. This was then dispatched, along with the tank, for some subtle freehand pin striping to Somerset's finest painter - Joeby over in Wells.

While the tank and 'guard were over with Joeby, Rob got on with the other 101 tasks he still had to do which included making (takes

a deep breath) the side number plate, the exhausts, the handlebars, the foot peg hangers, the battery box, the rear brake set up and bracket, shaving the forks and modifying the yokes. Whilst at the front he added a Nissin four pot caliper and linked it to a Brembo lever assembly to aid retardation - a Brembo assembly was also used for the clutch. To light his way a Bates headlight was acquired, again from eBay, and to complete the front end his son James bought him period grips and fork gaiters for Christmas.

Moving towards the rear of the bike, Larry, another useful mate, made the footpegs, exhaust tips and velocity stacks. The solo seat and springs were another eBay find, and finally arriving at the rear a one-off rear sprocket was machined to fit the Harley hub. The braking is again by Nissin, a two pot this time, again a Brembo assembly, and, finally, a 1950s American repro car rear light completes the picture.

That was it - everything was present and correct and, with a blur of spanners, the odd tap with a large hammer and probably a little swearing, everything was assembled to make sure it fitted, lined up and did what it was supposed to. Taking a step back to admire his handiwork he liked what he saw, and slinging his leg over he tilted it from side to side. Now Rob's a firm believer that less is more – 'it's light' he thought, but it could it be lighter still. Gazing over the bike he contemplated junking the lights and mudguard, but

decided he would need them, then Eureka! It hit him - using an old hot rod trick he took a drill and fired holes into anything he thought could take it including the engine cases, front sprocket cover, top engine mount, side number plate,levers, discs and struts to lighten a bike that already weighed little more than Kate Moss on a thirty day fast.

Great, he was happy - everything worked. Now it could all come apart again for the finishing touches and wiring. Scooby took the frame, 'bars, risers and number plate mount and powder coated

them satin black, and Nick Taylor satin polished all the stainless steel and alloy and rechromed the yokes.

Once everything was back in the garage and put back together again, Rob obtained and fitted some micro switches and turned the bike over to another friend who did a sterling job of creating light where there was once darkness and sparks were there was nothing, running all the wiring neatly out of sight.

That was it - everything done ship shape and Bristol

fashion. The big moment had finally arrived - would it run? Ignition on, petrol on, choke out, stab, rumble rumble - started first time on the button. Out onto the street, first, second, third and on up. It was light and quick, just what Rob envisioned right from the start of the build. Big grins all round! He had it on the road for all of a couple of months before someone made him an offer he couldn't refuse so he's building again watch this space.

To finish just a couple of points Rob would like to get across - no companies were involved in this build, just mates; everything is one-off or modified; and finally it was built with local talent - not pounds and dollars. So there! ⊗

Using an old hot rod trick he took a drill and fired holes into anything he thought could take it.

2009
Apr 16

ISSUE
115

OTHER BIKES FEATURED:
Triumph chopper, Suxuki café racer

THE BEST HARLEY
IN THE UK

I DON'T KNOW IF YOU KNOW, BUT HARLEY-DAVIDSON ACTUALLY DO A RANGE OF CUSTOM VERSIONS OF CERTAIN MODELS OF THEIR BIKES.

WORDS: NIK **PIX:** CLINTON@STUDIO-THREE.ORG **MODEL:** CANDICE

SPEC SHEET

ORIGINAL YEAR, MAKE & MODEL:

2005 Harley-Davidson CVO Screamin' Eagle Fat Boy

ENGINE:

2005 Harley-Davidson CVO Screamin' Eagle Fat Boy, 103 cubic inches, Screamin' Eagle Stroker flywheel assembly, Screamin' Eagle pistons, Screamin' Eagle big-bore cylinders, Screamin' Eagle heads, Screamin' Eagle teardrop air filter housing with Stage 1 air filter, heavy-duty 1.4 kilowatt starter, five speed gearbox, Yaffe Phantom exhausts

FRAME:

2005 Harley-Davidson CVO Screamin' Eagle Fat Boy, W&F 300 conversion, Harley-Davidson forward controls

SHARP END:

Avon Venom tyre, stock H-D CVO Screamin' Eagle Fat Boy wheel re-machined onto 4.25 highly polished rim, stock caliper, polished stock disc, lengthened braided steel brake line re-made to look like stock H-D brake line, 2" over Fat Boy forks, modified chrome upper sliders, 1" bars with concealed wiring, Ness mirrors

Back in 1998, they decided to allow a select few of their engineers and designers to come up with some fresh and exciting new ideas that would, eventually, lead to the creation of a small number of very special bikes.

These bikes have their origins rooted deep within the Mo Co's family of motorcycles it's true, but what makes them different from their day-to-day siblings is the way they're accessorised and painted, and the fact that they're fitted with more powerful engines than the 'cooking' models too. The first bike, built under the moniker of CVO or Custom Vehicle Operations, was unveiled a year later in 1999 and, since then, Harley have generally introduced two new CVO bikes every year. For 2009, they offer four machines – a CVO Springer Softail, a CVO Fat Bob, a CVO Ultra Classic Electra Glide and a CVO Road Glide, all of which are being

> **'All Mike's plans'd paid off and he now truly owned the best Harley-Davidson in the country and it was Harley-Davidson themselves who reckoned so - serious kudos!'**

built in limited numbers to maintain their exclusivity.

The bike you see here in front is, or rather was, also a CVO special. It's a 2005 CVO Screamin' Eagle Fat Boy, to give its full name, and it belongs to a gentleman by the name of Mike Collyer from Cheshunt in Hertfordshire. Of course, seeing as this is 100% Biker and we don't really do stock bikes, especially on the cover, it hasn't remained as the CVO guys built it – in fact, there's hardly a part that hasn't actually been modified or improved in one way or another.

The idea behind the bike was a simple one – Mike wanted to own the best Harley in the country. In 2005, you see, Harley-Davidson were ◐

2009
Apr 16

ISSUE
115

OTHER BIKES FEATURED:
Triumph chopper, Suxuki café racer

running a competition between all the HOG groups to find the best bike in the land. The rules were simple - any H-D was eligible as long as it had a stock frame and a stock engine and gearbox but, apart from that, the sky was the limit. Mike was good friends with Ashley Troop from Venom Cycles (www.vemoncycles. co.uk) in Hornchurch who was a dealer for legendary German aftermarket parts manufacturer and customiser Warneke & Faust, or W&F as they're commonly known. Mike had liked what he'd seen of theirs and so he and Ash got in touch with them about building what they hoped would indeed be the best Harley in England. What Mike wanted them to do was a little outside their usual remit but, after much

discussion, a plan was agreed on and Ash loaded up the brand new CVO Fat Boy that Mike'd just bought and headed out to Germany to drop it off. Incidentally, when he bought the CVO bike from Harley UK, Mike didn't dare tell them what he was going to do with it because he was afraid they wouldn't sell it to him if they knew – CVO bikes are so rare, you see, that Harley wouldn't have been impressed with the fact that he was going to cut up one of their most exclusive machines straight out of the shop.
You can see their point to a certain extent – if you're just going to rip a brand new bike to bits and change it beyond all recognition, they'd

probably argue, why do it with something as rare and desirable as a CVO when you could just as easily do it with a bog stock showroom model? Mike, though, knew exactly what he wanted and what he wanted was a CVO.

The plan was to build a Fat Boy that was like a Fat Boy, but more so. He didn't want a radical chopper or a bobber or anything like that, he wanted a Harley that was still recognisably a Harley – the Fat Boy, in his opinion, is the best-looking of the Harley range (and the CVO with its extra chrome and goodies even

'He's not a pot hunter and he's got nothing to prove - he knows his bike is mustard and that's good enough for him.'

more so) so it'd be daft to change it so much that it no longer looked like a Fat Boy, wouldn't it? Besides which, under the rules of the competition, the bike still had to have a stock frame so that effectively ruled out major structural modifications anyway.

That doesn't mean the bike hasn't been extensively modified though, oh no. Starting at the front, the stock hub was chopped from the stock wheel and re-worked into a highly polished four and a quarter inch rim with a 160 Avon Venom tyre, and the stock disc has been polished. The front caliper is a CVO four pot item with their silver finish and chrome inserts, the front mudguard is a W&F long-style one, and the forks that they both bolt to are two inch over length Fat Boy ones that have been so skillfully

done that they don't appear any different from stock, but subtly add to the bike's overall presence. The upper sliders have been modified to blend in better too and, while the yokes are the standard CVO ones, the 'bars aren't – the CVO inch and a quarter ones have been reduced to inch ones with internal wiring and fitted with Ness mirrors.

Behind the headstock sits the heart of the beast – a 103 cubic inch (nearly 1700cc) CVO Screamin' Eagle engine based on the stock 1450 Twin Cam, but with a Screamin' Eagle stroker crank and flywheel, Screamin' Eagle big bore barrels and pistons, Screamin Eagle heads and a Screamin' Eagle air filter housing with a Stage 1 air filter making up the bigger capacity and allowing it to breathe properly. The stock fuel-injection system has been retained and tweaked to suit, but the CVO 'pipes were deemed not sexy enough and so they've been replaced with Supertrapp Phantom exhausts by Paul Yaffe. The gearbox is a stock ◗

2009
Apr 16

ISSUE
115

OTHER BIKES FEATURED:
Triumph chopper, Suxuki café racer

BLUNT END:

W&F 300 swingarm with concealed wiring, lowered Harley-Davidson shock, H-D CVO Screamin' Eagle Fat Boy wheel machined to fit 11x18" highly polished rim, Pro-Fab rear brake light switch, modified W&F struts, modified belt guard, modified axle adjuster covers, Avon Venom 300 tyre, stock rear brake caliper with concealed LED marker light, polished stock disc, W&F side-mount number plate

TINWARE:

W&F long style front mudguard, stretched W&F tank with Landmark LED fuel gauge, lowered & heavily modified W&F seat, W&F rear mudguard, modified oil tank

ELECTRICS:

Modified stock loom, Headwinds headlight, Maximum LED sequential front indicators, Kuryakyn LED rear indicators & tail lights, Cyril Huze white LED 'plate light,

PAINT:

W&F to Screamin' Eagle design

POLISHING:

W&F

ENGINEERING:

Bike built by W&F (www. warneke-faust.com), Hot Toppers chrome bolt covers throughout

THANKS TO:

'Phil from riding it to the shoot; my wife Lesley for all her support; Ashley Troop for all his help; & Candice, my daughter, for modelling with it...'

H-D five speeder, and the starter has been uprated by CVO to a 1.4 kilowatt one in order to turn the larger capacity motor over.

Above this lusty pump sits a stretched W&F fuel tank with a Landmark LED fuel gauge and a mix of CVO and W&F dash and switches and whatnot. The seat behind it is an absolute work of art in itself – it's modeled on the CVO one that comes with the bike but is, of course, significantly wider than it because of the new 300 section back end (more on that in a mo'). The CVO seat comes with a very nicely-designed chromed rear edge panel done in a particularly hard to replicate style and copying this alone took four attempts to get just right. Mike has got a matching pillion seat for the bike too but, he feels, it looks so much better as a solo so it doesn't get bolted on often.

Back on with the tale. At the time W&F didn't actually do a 300 conversion (the biggest they offered was a 280) so everything for this build had to be made specially. The new extra-wide swingarm they made conceals all the wiring for the rear electrical components and cradles between its arms another much-modified wheel. Like the front, it's the stock CVO item cut from its original rim and machined to fit a new eleven inch wide eighteen inch highly polished rim and, again like the front, it's been so subtly done that it's not immediately apparent that it's not the standard hoop ... except, of course, for the fact that it's a hell

of a lot wider than a stock Fat Boy wheel. It too has a polished disc and a silver-finished CVO four pot caliper with natty chrome inserts, but the rear caliper, unlike the front, has been cleverly fitted with a tiny concealed LED marker light that, despite its size, kicks out a hell of a light and, at night, makes the polished rear wheel positively glow in the dark. A lowered Harley-Davidson shock gives the rear end the required stance and a widened (they only did 280 rears prior to this, remember?) W&F mudguard is supported by modified W&F struts, while both the belt guard and the axle adjuster covers have also felt the loving touch of the German craftsmen who constructed the bike too.

'CVO offered the 2005 Fat Boy in a choice of three colour schemes in the form of a two-tone paint scheme accented for the first time by Harley with a different one-of-a-kind metal-grind accent', it says in their bumf on the Internet. I'm assuming that means 'metallic paint' to you and me. The colour choices were Candy Cobalt and Starlight Black, Platinum Mist and Slate, and Electric Cherry and Vivid Black – Mike's bike came in that second scheme and W&F skillfully replicated it on all the new components. Everything that needed polishing (which was a hell of a lot, as you can see) was done in-house and, just eight weeks after they'd started, W&F wheeled the finished bike out into the German sunlight and stood back to admire their handiwork.

Back in the UK a short time later, Mike was gobsmacked – the bike looked a million dollars (although it didn't cost anywhere near that, obviously) and was just how he envisaged it. It flew through the early rounds of the H-D competition and, in the end after being judged

a select panel of expert judges from Harley-Davidson Europe, was awarded not one, but two of their top awards – 'Best Fat Boy' and, get this, 'Best Harley in the UK' too. All Mike's plans'd paid off and he now truly owned the best Harley-Davidson in the country and it was Harley-Davidson themselves who reckoned so – serious kudos! He now also owned a 2006 V-Rod too 'cos that was what first prize in the competition was, and had also picked up an all-expenses-paid luxury VIP trip to the Screamin' Eagle Drag Racing World Finals in Pomona in California too for winning 'Best Fat Boy' – not a bad haul for the first, and as it happens only, custom show his bike has been

entered in.

That's right – since the close of the competition four years ago, the Collyer CVO Screamin' Eagle Fat Boy hasn't really been seen out anywhere partly because Mike has, sadly, suffered from some serious health problems, and partly because … well, after winning accolades like that, a £20 trophy at a 'normal' custom show just doesn't hold any appeal for him. He's not a pot hunter and he's got nothing to prove – he knows his bike is mustard and that's good enough for him. Admirable self-control there, Mike - it would've been easy to have taken the bike out and cleaned up at just about every event he could've entered – and thankyou for bringing it out for us to photograph it. ✪

2009
June 11

ISSUE
117

OTHER BIKES FEATURED:
Café racer, XJ900, Hayabusa

THE ULTIMA(TE) ATTITUDE

WORDS: NIK **PIX:** CLINTON SMITH **MODEL:** KARINA HOLMES (WWW.KARINAHOLMES.CO.UK)

AS YOU MIGHT HAVE NOTICED WE'VE RUN A COUPLE OF BIKES BUILT BY SIMON HARRIS AT ATTITUDE CUSTOMS IN THE LAST SIX MONTHS OR SO – NAMELY HIS OWN LONG-FORKED ULTIMA AND CHRIS' SPORTSTER BOBBER.

SPEC SHEET

ENGINE:
Ultima 100 cubic inch, S&S Super E carb, Northwood Customs air-filter, one-off exhaust by Attitude Customs with Supertrapp cans, Roadmax six speed RSD gearbox with internal oil tank, BDL three inch primary, Crane Hi 4 ignition

FRAME:
Attitude Customs drop seat rigid, Northwood Customs forward controls, Attitude Customs battery box

SHARP END:
Taylormade Performance five spoke 8x18" billet split rim wheel, 240 Metzeler tyre, Beringer four pot brake, three inch over Suzuki GSX-R 1100 upside-down forks, one-off billet yokes by Attitude Customs, one-off 'bars by Attitude Customs/owner, Streamline six bearing internal throttle, Roland Stocker controls

T he thing is, though, while both of those bikes may well indeed have been built by the Southampton custom meister himself (he's going to love me for that ...) they weren't, if you like, Si Harris bikes – the kind of bikes that he's become famous ... no, notorious for building over the past ...umm ... quite a few years. You see, ever since he built 'Rent Boy', the first of his fat-wheelers to be seen in any bike magazine, from stuff just lying around in his garage, Mr Harris has earned himself a reputation for building motorcycles with front wheels so large they can almost be seen from space. To

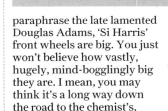

> **'Si Harris' front wheels are big. You just won't believe how vastly, hugely, mind-bogglingly big they are.'**

paraphrase the late lamented Douglas Adams, 'Si Harris' front wheels are big. You just won't believe how vastly, hugely, mind-bogglingly big they are. I mean, you may think it's a long way down the road to the chemist's, but that's just peanuts to a Si Harris front wheel'.

So, I think we've established that bikes built by him have large front wheels, haven't we? How is it, then, that the last two we've featured in this 'ere magazine had front hoops so normal they could be called Derek and work in an accounts office? What exactly is going on with the world? Well, fret ye not, those bikes were obviously an aberration, a blip on his mental landscape, because as you can plainly see the motorcycle here in front of you has a hee-owge front wheel and it was, of course, built by him. Hurrah! Okay, so the foremost hoop on this one isn't quite as mad as it could perhaps have been being as it's only ('only?') eight inches wide and is only

(there's that word again) fitted with a 260 section tyre, but it does mean that, without a doubt, this is a Si Harris bike and no mistake.

The owner, Neil Warner, a bike and custom car nut from Finchampstead in Berkshire, had seen Si's bikes at shows ❯

2009
June 11

ISSUE
117

OTHER BIKES FEATURED:
Café racer, XJ900, Hayabusa

BLUNT END:
Taylormade Performance five spoke 11x18" billet split rim wheel, 300 Metzeler tyre, Exile 'sprotor' sprocket brake

TINWARE:
Modified Demon Cycles fuel tank, one-off seat by Attitude Customs, one-off rear mudguard by Attitude Customs

ELECTRICS:
One-off loom by Steve

PAINT:
Revolution Custom Paints (01189 574577)

POLISHING:
PTS Polishing

ENGINEERING:
Bike built by Simon Harris at Attitude Customs (07758 241143 or www. attitude-customs.co.uk)

THANKS TO:
'Simon & Bill at Attitude Customs; & Graham at Revolution Custom Paint...'

over the years and loved the style of them so, when he had a choice of buying a new Harley or getting something with some real presence, he opted to ring Simon and commission him to build him a big-wheeled behemoth of his very own. After a quick chat on the 'phone, Neil traipsed down to Southampton to see him and they sat down and went through every detail of what was going to be built. It wasn't just a case of 'hand over the cash and come back in a year's time please' though - there was a fair amount of hands-on from Neil to get the bike to look exactly as he wanted. He went backwards and forwards to Southampton a lot and a fair amount was done by email too - Simon would send pictures through to Neil of what he'd done and things would be changed like, for example, the 'pipes. Originally they went for slash-cuts but, once they'd been made and fitted onto the bike, they really didn't look right so Si made up some short custom ones with Supertrapp silencers on the ends and, they both agreed, they were just the job. The bike obviously think so too because it runs a lot more smoothly with them

on. It was the same with the 'bars - Si made them three or four times before Neil was entirely happy with them. Since then the same design 'bars have appeared on other Attitude bikes - Neil said, laughing, 'I should have put a patent on them ...'

So what actually is the bike? Well, it's one of Attitude Customs' (the name Si works under now that he's turned full-time builder) trademark deep seat rigids, made by Simon's frame guru Bill, fitted with a set of three inch over GSX-R upside-down forks, held in Attitude billet yokes, and a pair of five spoke billet split rim wheels by, yep, you guessed it, Steve Taylor at Taylormade Performance. Simon and Steve have been working together now for more years than either of them

care to remember and it's rare these days to see a big-wheeled Attitude bike that isn't rolling on a set of Steve's hoops. As previously mentioned, the front one uses an eight inch wide rim (eighteen inch diameter) with a 260 tyre and the rear is an 11x18" with a 300 tyre. French brake specialists Beringer supplied the front stopper, and the rear is an Exile 'sprotor' which, roughly translated from the American, means 'sprocket brake' to you and me.

The powerplant that provides the motive power for the beast is a one hundred cubic inch (or 1638cc) Ultima with a Roadmax six speed right-side-drive gearbox with built-in oil tank hooked to the Ultima engine via a BDL three inch primary with a decorated belt. The carb's an S&S Super E, the 'filter's a Northwood Customs one and the ignition is by way of sparks generated by a Crane Hi4 unit. These Ultima engines seem to be appearing more and more

in customs in this country (this is the second one this issue!) and the reason for this that (a) they're competitively priced and (b) kick out a very healthy 115bhp and 115 ft/lbs of torque and so, as you can imagine, stonk on very nicely indeed.

Simon modified and stretched a Demon Cycles fuel tank that they got off the 'Net and made up the ultra-wide rear mudguard that covers the 300 section tyre, and then they and the frame were taken to Graham at Revolution Custom Paint (which you may or may not know was formerly Plastech) to be given the green/red/black/white paint scheme you see before you. Revolution also laid down the custom

'Looks like a fish, goes like a fish, steers like a cow'

green mix with gold metalflake on the spokes of the wheels, while Neil arranged for the rims to be powdercoated white and then rebuilt them using the countless coloured capheads you can see in the pictures. All the parts were then taken back to Simon at his workshop where he then nailed them together in a flurry of spanners.

The finished beast was unleashed just before the Bulldog in 2007 and, Neil says, it came out looking just as he visualised it. The flat seat makes it a lot more comfortable to ride than a conventional rigid ('cos yer arse is flat, see, not shoved into an angled gap) and, while the big Ultima motor has more get-up-and-go than an insulted celebrity, the combination of the big exotic Beringer front brake and the tres-sexy Exile rear 'un keep it well under control. Okay, so it handles like the proverbial shopping trolley compared with the latest generation of sports bikes (to quote Mr Adams again, 'looks like a fish, goes like a fish, steers like a cow'), but that's not the point of a bike like this, is it? The point of a bike like this is to be almost a caricature of a chopper, to be more in-yer-face than a pissed-up Sheffield Wednesday supporter, to be the Ultima(te) in Attitude, and it does this rather well - rather well indeed.

You'll notice that the completion date for this build was 2007 and, seeing as that was near two years ago, you can probably guess what's coming next, can't you? Yep, that's right, Neil's bike is for sale. He fancies a new toy, you see, and to fund that he needs to sell the Attitude. If

you can see yourself sitting in the saddle, hanging onto the 'bars when you whack open the internal throttle, and grinning like a loon as you do so, ring him on 07980 691434 but be aware – this is a top spec custom and serious offers only will be considered so don't go ringing up and trying to palm him off with three and a half pee, some bellybutton fluff and half a packet of Smarties, okay? I've already tried that and he wasn't having any of it. ⊗

IF IT AIN'T FAT IT AIN'T CUSTOM

WORDS: NIK
PIX: JOHN BRANDWOOD
MODEL: ANNIE NORRIS

THE WHOLE WORLD WANTS TO BE AMERICAN. IT'S SAD, I KNOW, BUT IT'S TRUE. JUST ABOUT EVERYTHING IN OUR EVERY DAY LIVES IS INFLUENCED ONE WAY OR ANOTHER BY THE MOST POWERFUL NATION ON THE PLANET – WHAT WE EAT, WHAT WE DRINK, THE WAY WE DRESS, THE CARS WE DRIVE, THE TELEVISION WE WATCH, THE MUSIC WE LISTEN TO, EVEN THE WAY WE HAVE SEX.

Anything that's come from America is seen as good ('cept, perhaps, the armaments directed at our troops in so-called 'friendly fire' incidents) and, it seems, all our major fashions and influences are taken from our cousins across The Pond. That's why we have white rappers, bling bling jewelry, McDonalds double cheese

burgers and chronic obesity. As bikers we're no better – we seem almost desperate to be seen to be the same as bikers Stateside. Look around any rally and you'll see folk wearing chaps, baseball caps and cowboy hats, tee-shirts

with slogans like 'If you can read this, the bitch fell off!', and Confederate flags on their cut-offs. There's even a section of our community that calls the people who lead their ride-outs 'road captains', and I've lost track of the number of times I've heard folk with thick regional accents talk about 'sickles', 'sleds', 'scooters' and 'bros'. Okay, so I get it that 'Easy Rider' had a major impact on the fledgling custom bike community when it first came out in 1969 but, honestly people, that was nearly forty years ago – have we not developed our own identity as British bikers in the four decades since? I have to admit that I'm perhaps as guilty as anyone as I'm a compulsive Converse All-Star wearer and I have been known, on one or two occasions (ahem), to don a baseball cap and sing along to, and be emotionally influenced by, the ❍

SPEC SHEET

ENGINE
1999 Suzuki GSX 1300R Hayabusa, Brocks Performance airbox modification, K&N air-filter, T&S drag clutch up-grade, Power Commander 3 USB ignition, Brocks Performance sidewinder drag 'pipe, NOS 50hp dry airbox shot nitrous oxide system, Earls braided oil & water lines

POWER OUTPUT
235bhp at rear wheel

FRAME
1999 Suzuki GSX 1300R Hayabusa, polished, FAT300 Custom Cycles spike footrests

SHARP END
Voodoo Fetish 2 chrome wheel, 120/70/17 tyre, single Galfer floating chrome disc, polished stock caliper, polished stock forks, Goodridge braided stainless steel brake lines, FAT300 Custom Cycles chromed billet alloy yokes, stock 'bars, FAT300 Custom Cycles chrome grips & spike ends, polished stock master-cylinders, chromed stock switchgear, Speed Hut blue glow clocks, FAT300 Custom Cycles chrome instrument surround

odd Steve Earle album but, hey, that doesn't make me a bad person, does it?

Of course, there are some good things to have come out of this peculiar obsession – if it wasn't for the influences of our Septic friends, then there would probably be no custom bike lifestyle in this country (or any other, come to think of it) or, if there was, it'd be one that identified by the fact that its adherents all wore black leather jackets covered in badges, ice-blue jeans (oh no, 'ang on, they're American too) and big boots with sea-boot socks. If it wasn't for the Yanks there'd've been no chops, no bobbers, no low-riders, no street sleepers, no drag bikes, no board-racers, no flat-trackers, no supermotos (you might've thought they were actually French but, no, they're originally American too). We might have streetfighters (because, like café racers, they're a particularly British invention) and ... umm ... that's about it. Rats possibly?

Surprisingly then, given that almost everything from the States is seen as being hip and happening, it's a bit odd that this style of American bike – the one in which this 'ere Hayabusa has been built – hasn't caught on quite as much

Given that almost everything from the States is seen as being hip and happening, it's a bit odd that this style of American bike hasn't caught on quite as much as others have.

SPEC SHEET

BLUNT END

FAT300 Custom Cycles 15" over-stock chrome swingarm, 2lb NOS bottle holder, chromed solid show strut, Voodoo Fetish 2 chrome wheel with 360/30/18 Veerubber Monster tyre, laser cut Hayabusa logo stainless disc, polished stock caliper, adjustable alloy torque arm, D&D chrome chain, Voodoo chrome sprocket

TINWARE

Triple chrome plated stock front mudguard/fairing/petrol tank/tail-piece by H2OCycles (Florida), FAT300 Custom Cycles chrome seat/blue ostrich skin seat (for riding)

ELECTRICS

Stock loom & headlight, integrated LED tail-light/indicators, blue LED under body & swingarm lights

POLISHING

M&G Polishers, Halifax

ENGINEERING

Making things fit after chroming & aftermarket parts that never fit by owner (many cut finger tips & sore hands - they still hurt now!)

THANKS TO

'George at FAT300 Custom Cycles (www.fat330customcycles.com); H2O Cycles (www.h2ocycles.com); Brocks Performance (www.brocksperformance.com); John at Crossbow Calendars; Lee at MFN in Nottingham; my wife Jayne and daughter Sophie for putting up with my endless days in the garage & being woken in the early hours by the man from UPS with deliveries from America ...'

This process took eighteen months and loads of emails chasing parts back and forth which, he says, really did his head in.

as others have. In the US, taking a stock Japanese sports bike, putting a back wheel the size of Washington State into it and then generally blinging the hell out of it is huge but, in this country, bar one or two examples it'd almost unheard of. I have to admit that when you see bikes done this well I can't quite see why the style hasn't taken off – yes, they're still plastic bikes, as their detractors will no doubt sneer, but this thing just has so much presence it's ridiculous.

Jon Boulby bought a stock 1999 Hayabusa about four years ago and almost immediately started to change bits here and there on it. He polished the frame and lots of other parts and added chrome wheels and a longer swingarm and it appeared in the 2003 Crossbow Calendar. That was the start of something big. He was very

happy with it as it was, but it lacked just a little something – he didn't know quite what that little something was, but he knew that it lacked it nonetheless.

Then one day while idly browsing the 'Web, he happened upon the website

of H2O Cycles in Jacksonville, Florida and saw the completely chromed Hayabusa that they'd done. That was it, that's what his 'Busa lacked – more shininess than Matt Lucas' freshly buffed bone dome. He emailed the guys there and asked them about the process and, happy with their replies, stripped the bodywork off his bike and posted it over to them. Sounds simple enough, doesn't it? It wasn't – this process took eighteen months and loads of emails chasing parts back and forth which, he says, really did his head in. And it didn't end when he got everything back either - every panel needed careful grinding back so that they'd fit together again. The process of chroming plastic is quite involved,

you see - the stock panel is first sprayed with a brass spray which can then be charged at low voltage to get the copper (the first layer of the three in triple chrome plating) to stick to it. Once this is achieved the nickel and, finally, the chrome top coats are fairly straight forward but, after they have been plated,
some of the leading edges where the panels
fit back together on the bike are all bubbled and rough, and this takes a lot of patience and a steady hand to get them back to how they were. And, of course, there's now no bend in the panels as they are now sandwiched with metal.

The frame he polished himself as he did with most of the small parts, but gave the larger parts to the professionals - they can do a better job on stuff like forks and calipers than anyone at home can. M&G Metal Polishing in Halifax were the people contracted to do it and they made a bonzer job of it too. All the billet parts (levers, fork caps, grips etc) came from a variety of companies in the States and are all (a) top class and (b) a lot cheaper than anyone selling them over here could do them for (and that was including shipping costs). In fact, Jon says, the only stuff on the bike that came from over here is the air in the tyres.

He then fitted a 240 rear section tyre kit to the freshly polished and chromed bike and ran it for a year or so like

that but, he felt, it didn't look quite right. Another evening's 'Net searching turned up a guy called George who runs an outfit called FAT 300 Custom Cycles in Florida. He offers a Monster Rear End kit for most late Jap sports bikes and gives you a choice of 300, 330 or 360 rear wheels. Jon knew it had to be a 360 – anything else would be a little ghey – and soon became friends with George to the extent of meeting up with him and his wife at Biketoberfest last year.

The Monster FAT kits are designed so that no cutting or tweaking to the frame is necessary! The kits are model specific but, if you want one for something that's not a full line production model, they can fabricate you one too. They're available in raw, polished, chromed, candy chromed or

power-coated finishes and are comprehensive – you get the swingarm (8-16" over, depending on the wheel you choose), the front and rear wheels (so that they match), the jackshaft to transfer the power from the gearbox to the wheel, a jackshaft cover, the 300, 330 or 360FAT series rear tyre (and a front too), both chains (sprocket to jackshaft and jackshaft to wheel), a new brake line, a new rear sprocket, a new torque arm and, of course, axles and spacers for whichever wheels you choose (they stock a full range of RC, PM or Voodoo Industry Wheels). On top of that you can also go for a solid ◗

The Monster FAT kits are designed so that no cutting or tweaking to the frame is necessary! The kits are model specific but, if you want one for something that's not a full line production model, they can fabricate you one too.

The heart of the bike hasn't been ignored either – the 1999 GSX 1300R motor has been treated to a Brocks Performance airbox modification and a K&N air-filter to allow it to breathe properly.

strut to replace your shock or a heavy-duty spring, lowering links, a bracket to hold a nitrous oxide bottle, a built-in air tank to power an Air-Ride shock (if you have one), and/or seriously blingy swingarm adjuster blocks. Jon's went for the basic 360 kit with a fifteen inch over swingarm and a Voodoo Fetish 2 wheel, and added a nitrous bottle bracket to hold his nitrous bottle (natch), a solid rear disc with the Hayabusa logo cut in and a solid rear strut which, he says, along with the fat wheel and the long 'arm, makes it handle like it's pulling a caravan, but looks

the ab-so-lute dog's danglies.

Up front there's another Voodoo Fetish 2 wheel. One of the front discs (and caliper, of course) has been removed for that pukka drag-strip look and the disc itself replaced with a chromed Galfer wavy one. The forks have been polished and slotted into FAT300 Custom Cycles billet yokes, and the 'bars given chromed switchgear and FAT300 Custom Cycles grips and 'bar 'ends that match the footrests.

The heart of the bike hasn't been ignored either – the 1999 GSX 1300R motor has been treated to a Brocks Performance airbox modification and a K&N air-filter to allow it to breathe properly, a multi-programmable

Power Commander III ignition box to control the sparks and a Brocks Performance sidewinder drag 'pipe to get the burnt hydrocarbons out sharpish. It sounds like the Devil himself with that 'pipe and, with a fifty brake horsepower shot of nitrous oxide waiting at the touch of a button (and a T&S drag clutch up-grade to control it), it goes like the Old Chap is after you himself too.

It's taken four long years of work to get the bike to the stage you see here in front of you but it's been, Jon says, worth it; 'The trouble is when you chrome or polish one part, then everything else looks so boring and dirty. If you start, where do you stop? The more you do, the better it looks ... it's Catch 22', he laughs.

He's well pleased with the bike – it's in this year's Crossbow Calendar in all its full-chrome glory and it's in Nick Sanders' 'Biker Britain' book and on his DVD that's just been aired on Men & Motors. It always draws in a crowd wherever they go and while it's not the most comfortable ride and, as he said earlier, handles like you're pulling a caravan, the buzz you get from people when they see it makes up from all the polishing and pain. Mind you, that's not to say that he isn't already planning his next project - a ZX1400 Kawaski with a 360 kit and 'a bit of chrome and a nice paint job'. We look forward to seeing it, Jon, and a few more US-influenced street bikes too. ⊗